shop image graphics

P·I·E BOOKS

P·I·E BOOKS

Villa Phoenix Suite 301, 4-14-6 Komagome,
Toshima-ku, Tokyo 170-0003 Japan
Tel: +81-3-3940-8302 Fax: +81-3-3576-7361
e-mail: editor@piebooks.com
        sales@piebooks.com

ISBN4-89444-145-4 C3070

Printed in Japan

659. 157 SHO

332736

CONTENTS

9-92

住 Shelter ●

CONTENTS

93-152

 衣 Clothing ●

CONTENTS

153-232

食 Food ●

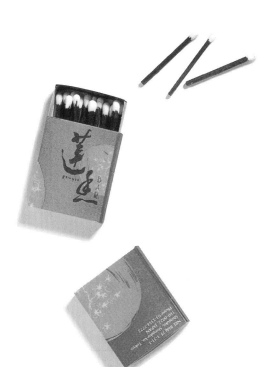

序 文

世界はさまざまなイメージで構成されている。衣類、料理、音楽、映画、本、家具、食器、化粧品…。わたしたちの身のまわりにあるものは、誰かの頭の中に浮かんだあるイメージが、さまざまな人々の手によって創造され、それが商品という形になって市場に供給されたものだ。だがそうやって誕生した商品も、具体的な販売戦略やコンセプトなくしては、消費者の購買意欲を刺激することも集客力を高めることもできない。商品イメージの伝達が消費者に対して十分に行われなかった商品には、ひっそりとこの世から姿を消していくという運命が待ち受けているだけである。

そんな中、販売戦略の一環として注目されているのが、人々が直接商品を購入、あるいは時間を消費する空間である「店」というメディアを活用した、商品のイメージコントロールである。「店」を単なる商品を陳列・販売する「箱」としてではなく、商品と消費者をつなぐコミュニケーションの「場」としてとらえ、五感に訴えかける魅力的な店づくりを実現させれば、おのずと人々は集い商品や時間が消費されていく。実際に、女性にとっての心地よさをテーマに衣食住にかかわる商品をプロデュースして販売するライフスタイルショップ、音楽とファッションの融合を目指すブティック、非日常的な空間の中で無国籍料理を提供するレストランなど、魅力あふれるショップが続々と誕生し、人々を引きつけている。

ショップで扱う商品のトータルイメージを、どう「視覚的」に表現・演出すれば、人々の記憶に残る店づくり、すなわちビジネスを成功させることができるのか。本書では、その秘密を、店舗のファサード、内観、ロゴデザイン、そのロゴを使用したオリジナルの販売促進ツールを、ショップ別に紹介することによって解き明かしていく。

ショップ経営にかかわる人にとって、イメージという目に見えないものをデザイナーやプランナーに的確に伝え、具体的な形に仕上げていくのは非常に困難な作業だ。クライアントの持つイメージを理解し、自らの感性とアイデア、そしてさまざまな技術を駆使して目に見える形にしていくデザイナーやプランナーもまた然り。そうした困難極まるハードルをいくつも乗り越え、魅力的な店づくりを成功させたショップを、今回こうしてみなさまにご紹介できることは誠に光栄である。

最後に、本書制作にあたりご協力をいただいたショップ関係者、広告・デザイン関係者のみなさまに感謝の意を表したい。

ピエ・ブックス編集部

FOREWORD

The world we live in is composed of various images—clothes, cuisine, music, movies, books, furniture, tableware, cosmetics, and so on. The things around us began as images in someone's head, took form as a result of creative input from various people, and were then supplied to us as products. Without concrete sales strategies and concepts however, products conceived in this way cannot attract the consumer or stimulate their desire to purchase. If insufficient effort is made to convey a product image to the consumer, the chances are that product will simply fade quietly into obscurity.

One aspect of sales strategy currently attracting considerable attention is that of product image control via the medium of the "shop," i.e. the space where people actually buy products, or pass time. If the "shop" can be more than a "box" in which merchandise is displayed and sold, that is if it can be a venue for communication linking product and consumer, and if that shop appeals successfully to the five senses, people will be drawn to it and both products and time will be consumed as a matter of course. Retail facilities with strong appeal—such as life-style shops that produce and sell items meeting the basic needs of food, shelter and clothing, with a focus on creating a comfortable environment for female shoppers; boutiques that endeavor to fuse music and fashion; and restaurants serving food that defies national boundaries, in surroundings divorced from the everyday—are appearing in rapid succession and successfully luring people through their doors.

The question is, how do we visually express or present a total image for a shop's merchandise that people will remember, in other words that will ensure success for the business? In this book we reveal how it can be done, by showing the facades, interior views, logos and original sales promotion tools employing those logos of a selection of shops.

For the person operating a shop, communicating accurately something as intangible as an image to a designer or planner and endowing that image with a concrete form is extremely difficult. The same goes for the designer or planner, who must understand the image the client has in mind, incorporate their own sensibilities and ideas about what will work best, and employ various skills to create a tangible form for that image. It is truly an honor to be able to present to you in this volume a selection of shops that have overcome several of these most difficult hurdles to successfully create the kind of premises that attract consumers.

Lastly, I would like to thank everyone involved with the shops in this book and from the worlds of advertising and design that cooperated in its production.

The P·I·E Books Editorial staff

Editorial Notes

クレジット フォーマット　Credit Format

A.	店舗名の日本語表記	Japanese reading of store name
B.	店舗名のアルファベット表記	Alphabetized reading of store name
C.	店舗の所在国	Country of location
D.	店舗の所在地	Address
E.	制作スタッフクレジット	Creative staff
F.	店舗の正式名称	Store name
G.	業種（取り扱い商品）内容	Product types
H.	店舗紹介文	Store description

A. ● エアポート・アクタス

B. ● OSAKA AIRPORT ACTUS　Japan

C.

D. 大阪府豊中市蛍池西町3-555 大阪国際空港（伊丹）4F
4F Osaka Airport, 3-555 Nishi-machi Hotarugaike Toyonaka-shi Osaka

E. ● AF：㈱アクタス Actus
CD：大重 亨 Toru Oshige／伊東裕子 Yuko Ito（1）
D：森 曼好 Nobuyoshi Mori（1）
DF：アクタス企画室 Actus Advertising Division

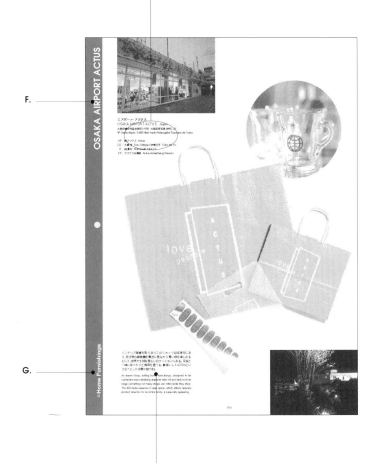

F.

G.

H.

制作スタッフ クレジット表記　Creative Staff

A:	ショップ設計者	Architect in charge
AF:	建築設計事務所	Architectural Firm
CD:	クリエイティブ・ディレクター	Creative Director
AD:	アート・ディレクター	Art Director
LD:	ロゴ・デザイナー	Logo Designer
D:	デザイナー	Designer
P:	カメラマン	Photographer
I:	イラストレーター	Illustrator
CW:	コピーライター	Copywriter
DF:	グラフィックデザイン事務所	Design Firm

※上記以外の制作スタッフの呼称は、略さずに記載しています。
Full names of all others involved in the creation/production of the work.

※制作スタッフクレジット内で「Photographer」として記載されている方で、特に作品との照合番号がない方は同ページで紹介している店舗の写真を撮影されたカメラマンになります。
Except where indicated by a photo reference number after the photographer's name, all photos on the same page were taken by the architectural photographer.

※制作スタッフクレジット内で記載している会社名、個人名のアルファベット表記は、基本的に頭文字のみ大文字それ以外は小文字で表記を統一しています。
All alphabetized names are indicated in initial caps.

※情報提供者の意向によりクレジットデータの一部を記載していないものがあります。
Please note that some credit data has been omitted at the request of the submittor.

※本書に掲載している店舗写真、販促ツール、商品、店名、住所等は、すべて2000年7月時点での情報になりますのでご了承ください。
All in store-related information, including photography, promotional items, products, store name, and address are accurate as of July 2000.

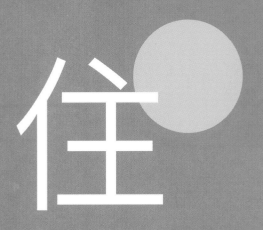

住

Shelter

生活＆服飾雑貨店と複合ショップ
Living / Fashion Accessories and Combination Shops

- ● 家具・リビング用品　Home Furnishings
- ● 家庭用品　Housewares
- ● 日用品　Household Goods
- ● 食器　Tableware
- ● 化粧品　Cosmetics / Toiletries
- ● 栄養補給剤　Nutritional Supplement
- ● めがね　Optical Goods
- ● 服飾雑貨　Accessories
- ● アクセサリー　Jewelry
- ● 文具　Stationery
- ● 炭　Charcoal
- ● 本　Books
- ● 土産品　Souvenirs
- ● 旅行用品　Travel Goods
- ● 手作り雑貨　Handmade Goods
- ● おもちゃ　Toys
- ● 美容室　Beauty Salon

etc.

イルムス　ILLUMS　Japan

福岡県福岡市博多区下川端町3-1 スーパーブランドシティ4F
4F Super Brand City, 3-1 Shimokawabata-cho Hakata-ku
Fukuoka-shi Fukuoka

A：加田晴俊　Harutoshi Kada
AF：KADA空間設計事務所　Kada Three-dimensions

自然との共存の中、ナチュラルな素材を存分に活かした
インテリア小物や雑貨を積極的に取り入れ、清々しくや
さしい生活を楽しむ北欧のモダンスタイルを日本人に向
けて提案。グラフィックデザインに取り入れられている
「イルムスブルー」と呼ばれる水色が美しい。

Scandinavian modern home furnishings made with natural
materials offer a fresh and gentle touch to Japanese living. The
"Illums Blue" featured in the graphics has a sky-like beauty.

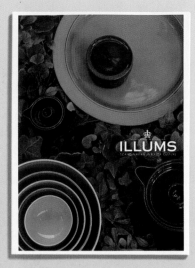

Tea party

Freshly baked cookies and tarts with splendid aroma of tea
are surely one of life's greatest temptations.

家での時間を楽しむ生活に、ティータイムの習慣は欠かせないものになります。
コーヒーや紅茶に手作りのクッキーやケーキを添えて、
友人たちと午後のひとときを過ごす。そのためにちょっと上等で、
自分の趣味を表現できるテーブルウェアを充実させることは、スカンジナビアの人々にとって、
とても大切で、また大きな楽しみと言えます。
その気になってあれこれ眺めると、ティーパーティーのテーブルトップも、
ひとつの部屋に負けないほどのデザインを楽しめる空間であることがわかります。

Candle Light

There is something spiritual how a candlelight
illuminates the space.
The overall impression entirely depends
upon one's state of mind.

ミニマックス　MINIMAX　Australia
582 Burke Road, Camberwell, Victoria 3124

A： アンディ・トムソン　Andy Thomson
AF： トムソン・リリー　Thomson Lilley
CD, AD, D, I： フィル・エレット　Phil Ellett
DF： コッツォリーノ・エレット・デザイン・ディビジョン
Cozzolino Ellett Design D'Vision

商品引換券　Gift Voucher

『ミニマックス』はスタイリッシュなミニ・デパート。色々なシンボルが買い物客を新鮮なコンテンポラリーイメージの売り場へ導く。

Minimax is a stylish mini-department store. Icons direct shoppers to the retail spaces, while creating a fresh, contemporary image.

ザ·コンランショップ
THE CONRAN SHOP   Japan
東京都新宿区西新宿3-7-1 新宿パークタワー 3-4F
3-4F Shinjuku Park Tower,
3-7-1 Nishi-Shinjuku Shinjuku-ku Tokyo

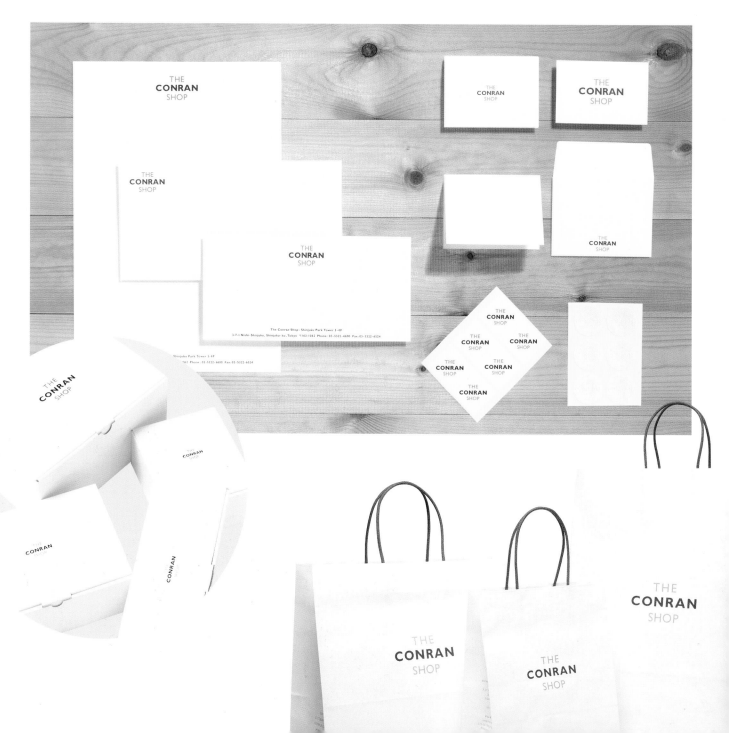

イギリスのデザイナー、テレンス・コンラン卿によって選ばれた物、デザインされたインテリア用品を扱う。菓子、石けん、時計、エプロンなど、生活全般に関わる様々なプロダクトが手に入る都会的な空間。

Sweets, soaps, clocks, aprons — a wide variety of products related to all aspects of living selected and/or designed by English designer Sir Terrance Conran, offered in an urban setting.

エアポート・アクタス
OSAKA AIRPORT ACTUS Japan

大阪府豊中市蛍池西町3-555 大阪国際空港(伊丹)4F
4F Osaka Airport, 3-555 Nishi-machi Hotarugaike Toyonaka-shi Osaka

AF：㈱アクタス Actus
CD：大重 亨 Toru Oshige / 伊東裕子 Yuko Ito (1)
 D：森 曼好 Nobuyoshi Mori (1)
DF：アクタス企画室 Actus Advertising Division

インテリア雑貨を取り扱うこのショップは空港内にあり、飛行機の離発着を間近に見ながら買い物を楽しめるという、世界でも類を見ないロケーションにある。家族と一緒にゆったりと商品を選べる、直線にして420mという広々とした空間が魅力的。

An airport shop, selling home furnishings, designed to let customers enjoy watching airplanes take-off and land at close range (something not many shops can offer) while they shop. The 420-meter expanse of open space, which affords leisurely product selection for an entire family, is especially appealing.

ボダム ショップ　bodum Shop　Japan

東京都渋谷区猿楽町28-13

28-13 Sarugaku-cho Shibuya-ku Tokyo

AF, DF： ピー デザイン　Pi Design

オーガナイズド・リビング　Organized Living　USA

CD： パトリス・アイルツ・ジューブ　Patrice Eilts-Jube
AD： ペギィ・レイリィ　Peggy Reilly
 P： スコット・ヘプラー　Scott Hepler
CW： ウェンディ・クライン　Wendy Klein
DF： イート・アドバタイジング＆デザイン
　　 Eat Advertising and Design

値札　Price Tag

『オーガナイズド・リビング』の「クリスマス宣伝キャンペーン 1999」のために制作されたツール。このキャンペーンは、容器類と同様にギフト用ラッピングペーパー、リボンを含むクリスマス用パッケージの宣伝販売に的を合わせてある。

Tools created for the Organized Living Holiday Promotional Campaign 1999 holiday season. The campaign focuses on promoting sales of holiday packaging, which includes giftwraps and bows as well as containers.

オーディニング＆レダ　ORDNING & REDA　Japan

東京都渋谷区代官山町20-23 ブラース代官山1F
1F La Place de Daikanyama, 20-23 Daikanyama-cho
Shibuya-ku Tokyo

ポストカード　Post Card

ポストカード　Post Card

ポストカード　Post Card

DMのデザインと連動したウィンドウ・ディスプレイが、
毎月テーマごとに変わるスウェーデン生まれの文具店。
「整理整頓」を意味する店名どおり、色別に商品が陳列さ
れ、実用的かつ目でも楽しめるショップになっている。

Direct-mail advertising and window displays reflect the
changing monthly themes of this Swedish stationery store. In
keeping with the store name, meaning "orderly and tidy,"
product displays are grouped by color — both functional and
visually delightful.

フランフラン　Franc franc　Japan
東京都世田谷区奥沢15-26-16 自由が丘マスト3F
3F Jiyugaoka Mast, 15-26-16 Okusawa Setagaya-ku Tokyo

CD： 永倉智彦　Tomohiko Nagakura (1)
AD, D： 青葉淑美　Yoshimi Aoba (1)
AD： 水野 学　Manabu Mizuno
D： 原田幸子　Sachiko Harada
　　宮島啓輔　Keisuke Miyajima
　　小山奈々子　Nanako Koyama
P： 小野寺幸浩　Yukihiro Onodera (1)
I： サチ　Sachi
CW： 河津典子　Noriko Kawazu
DF： グッドデザインカンパニー　Good Design Company
　　㈱サン・アド　Sun-Ad Co., Ltd. (1)

ショップカード　Shop Card

Franc franc is a home-furnishing store, offering you an idea for a fabulous habitation. Our underling concept is "casual stylish", and we would help you to make your habitation a real groovy one, well designed in a contemporary style, not too much, but in a very casual way.

Franc franc

Franc franc is a home-furnishing store, offering you an idea for a fabulous habitation. Our underling concept is "casual stylish", and we would help you to make your habitation a real groovy one, well designed in a contemporary style, not too much, but in a very casual way.

「カジュアル・スタイル」をキーワードに、このショップが制作・販売する家具や生活雑貨を取り入れた、普段の生活が心地よくなる居住空間づくりを提案。カラフルな商品や女性が喜びそうなグラフィックツールは、見ているだけで楽しい気分になれる。

"Casual-style" home furnishings produced and sold to provide more comfortable everyday living. Colorful products and graphics that particularly appeal to women are delightful just to look at.

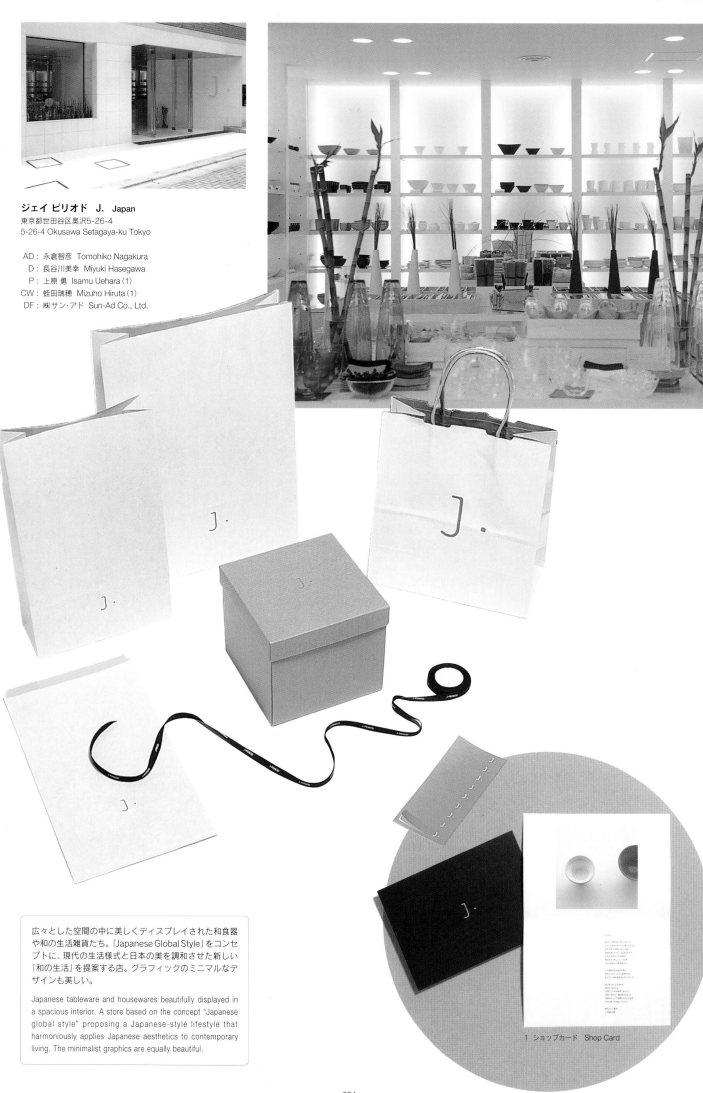

ジェイ ピリオド J. Japan

東京都世田谷区奥沢5-26-4
5-26-4 Okusawa Setagaya-ku Tokyo

AD： 永倉智彦 Tomohiko Nagakura
D： 長谷川美幸 Miyuki Hasegawa
P： 上原 勇 Isamu Uehara (1)
CW： 蛭田瑞穂 Mizuho Hiruta (1)
DF： ㈱サン・アド Sun-Ad Co., Ltd.

広々とした空間の中に美しくディスプレイされた和食器
や和の生活雑貨たち。「Japanese Global Style」をコンセ
プトに、現代の生活様式と日本の美を調和させた新しい
「和の生活」を提案する店。グラフィックのミニマルなデ
ザインも美しい。

Japanese tableware and housewares beautifully displayed in
a spacious interior. A store based on the concept "Japanese
global style" proposing a Japanese-style lifestyle that
harmoniously applies Japanese aesthetics to contemporary
living. The minimalist graphics are equally beautiful.

1 ショップカード Shop Card

アンド エー　&A.　Japan

東京都渋谷区宇田川町28-3
28-3 Udagawa-cho Shibuya-ku Tokyo

A： 吉井正生　Masaki Yoshii
AD, D： 草刈千絵　Chie Kusakari
AF, DF： ㈱サザビー　Sazaby Inc.

都会で働く女性が仕事の行き帰りに気軽に立ち寄って、服、生活雑貨、アロマオイルなどを購入できる店内は、清潔感あふれている。グリーンをテーマカラーにしたグラフィックスも、女性の生活を応援するショップらしくやさしいイメージで統一されている。

"Clean" defines the interior of a store customers can stop by on their way to or from work to pick up necessities ranging from clothes, household goods and aromatic oils, to garden supplies. The graphic design, with green as the principal color, reinforces the gentle image of a shop that supports women's lifestyles.

掌 GINZA TANAGOKORO Japan

東京都中央区銀座1-8-15
1-8-15 Ginza Chuo-ku Tokyo

「備長炭でつくる、新しい和のライフスタイルの提案」を
コンセプトに、マイナスイオン効果や消臭効果の高い備
長炭を利用したオリジナル商品を扱う店内には、空気を
浄化したヒーリングルームも併設。白、黒、オレンジ色を
配したグラフィックが炭の美を引き立たせている。

A shop offering original products made of Bincho charcoal,
known for its negative ion producing and deodorizing effects,
designed to present "a new Japanese lifestyle" includes a
healing room with purified air. The black, white and orange color
scheme of the graphics sets off the beauty of the charcoal.

グルメ・オーガニックス　Gourmet Organix　UK

North Lynton, Devon

CD, AD： ポール・ウエスト　Paul West
　　　　 ポーラ・ベンソン　Paula Benson
　　D： クリス・ヒルトン　Chris Hilton
　　DF： フォーム　Form

ポストカード　Post Card

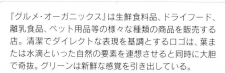

『グルメ・オーガニックス』は生鮮食料品、ドライフード、
離乳食品、ペット用品等の様々な種類の商品を販売する
店。清潔でダイレクトな表現を基調とするロゴは、葉ま
たは水滴といった自然の要素を連想させると同時に大胆
で奇抜。グリーンは新鮮な感覚を引き出している。

Gourmet Organix offers a diverse range of products including
fresh and dry foods, clothing, pet supplies and baby food. Based
on a clean, direct approach, the logo suggests elements of
nature such as a leaf or water droplet, whilst being bold and
confident. Green evokes a sense of freshness.

フリーズ ショップ
FREE'S SHOP　Japan
東京都渋谷区神宮前6-12-18
6-12-18 Jingumae Shibuya-ku Tokyo

AF：イデー Idée
Interior Designer：田沼広子　Hiroko Tanuma

カフェ＆ブティックの複合ショップ。カフェ内にはDJによる音楽が流れ、自由に閲覧できる洋書や洋雑誌が置かれている。テレビモニターではコレクション映像を流すなど、ファッションとカルチャーの融合を目指している。

A combination café/boutique proposing the fusion of fashion and culture. The café offers Western books and magazines for perusal and DJ-played music, while television monitors show the fashion collections.

コースター　Coaster

マディ　Madu　Japan

東京都渋谷区神南1-8-19 イニビル
Ini-Bldg., 1-8-19 Jinnan Shibuya-ku Tokyo

AF： ㈱ファッション須賀　Fashion Suga Co., Ltd.
D： 飯田 淳　Jun Iida
DF： シャワーズ　Showers Co., Ltd.

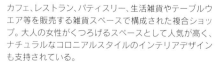

カフェ、レストラン、パティスリー、生活雑貨やテーブルウ
エア等を販売する雑貨スペースで構成された複合ショッ
プ。大人の女性がくつろげるスペースとして人気が高く、
ナチュラルなコロニアルスタイルのインテリアデザイン
も支持されている。

A combination café, restaurant, bakery, housewares and
tablewares variety store, popular as a place where women can
relax. The natural colonial-style design is unaffectedly pleasant.

ドゥ・セー deux C Japan
東京都目黒区自由が丘1-17-14
1-17-14 Jiyugaoka Meguro-ku Tokyo

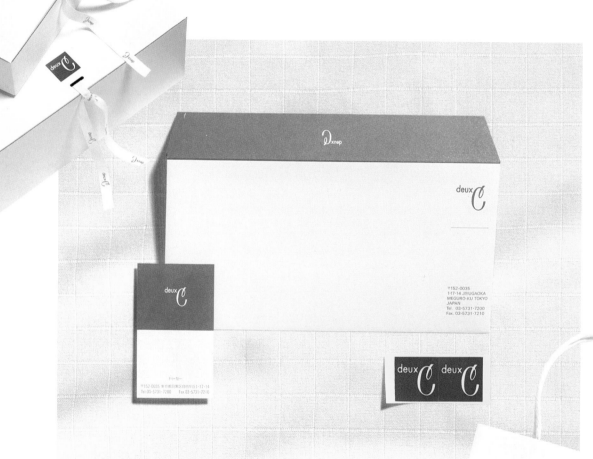

オリジナルのファブリック、食器、リラクシングウエアを
扱うこの店では、普段使いにぴったりな商品を、キッチ
ン、リビングなど様々なシチュエーション別に提案。お
しゃれなのに気取らない店の雰囲気を、グラフィックに
反映させている。

Original fabrics, tableware, and at-home wear displayed in
kitchen, living and other home settings perfectly matched to
the product uses. The stylish yet unpretentious atmosphere
is expressed in the graphics as well.

ユニッツ　units Japan

東京都目黒区自由が丘2-15-20
2-15-20 Jiyugaoka Meguro-ku Tokyo

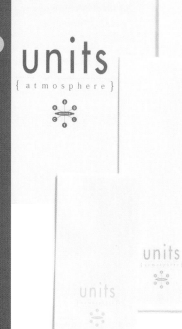

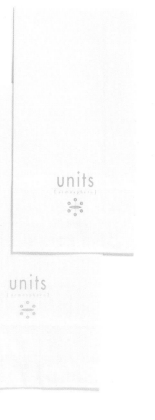

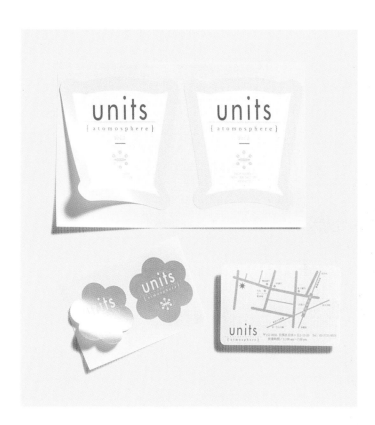

キッチン、バスルーム、寝室などで使われる、デザイン
性と機能性を兼ね備えた、ちょっとおしゃれでかわいい
日用雑貨が所狭しと並ぶ店内は、まるでおもちゃ屋のよ
うな楽しさ。カラフルな商品とイメージ統一されたグラ
フィックツールのかわいさも目を引く。

Well-designed, functional kitchen, bathroom, bedroom, and
other household goods that are also a touch fancy and cute,
line the store interior with the fun of a toy store. Cute
graphics designed to compliment the colorful array of
products are also eye-catching.

カタログ　Catalog

モモハウス　MOMO HOUSE　Japan

東京都目黒区自由が丘2-15-20 メイブルツインビル2F
2F Maple Twin-Bldg., 2-15-20 Jiyugaoka Meguro-ku Tokyo

CD：　脇 淳朗　Junro Waki
AD, D：　脇 理恵　Rie Waki
P：　中嶋良勝　Yoshikatsu Nakajima (1)
Stylist：　菊池美咲　Misaki Kikuchi
I, CW：　成田朋代　Tomoyo Narita
DF：　ヒラメキッズ　Hiramekids

「ナチュラル×シンプル×スタイリッシュ」を3本柱に、オリジナル家具の製造およびショップ構成を実践。どんなテイストにもコーディネイトできる、飽きのこないデザイン＋カジュアルプライスの家具が幅広い層にアピールしている。

Original-production furniture and a retail store based on the formula "natural × simple × stylish." Basic furniture that coordinates with any decor offered at a reasonable price appeals to wide range of people and tastes.

034

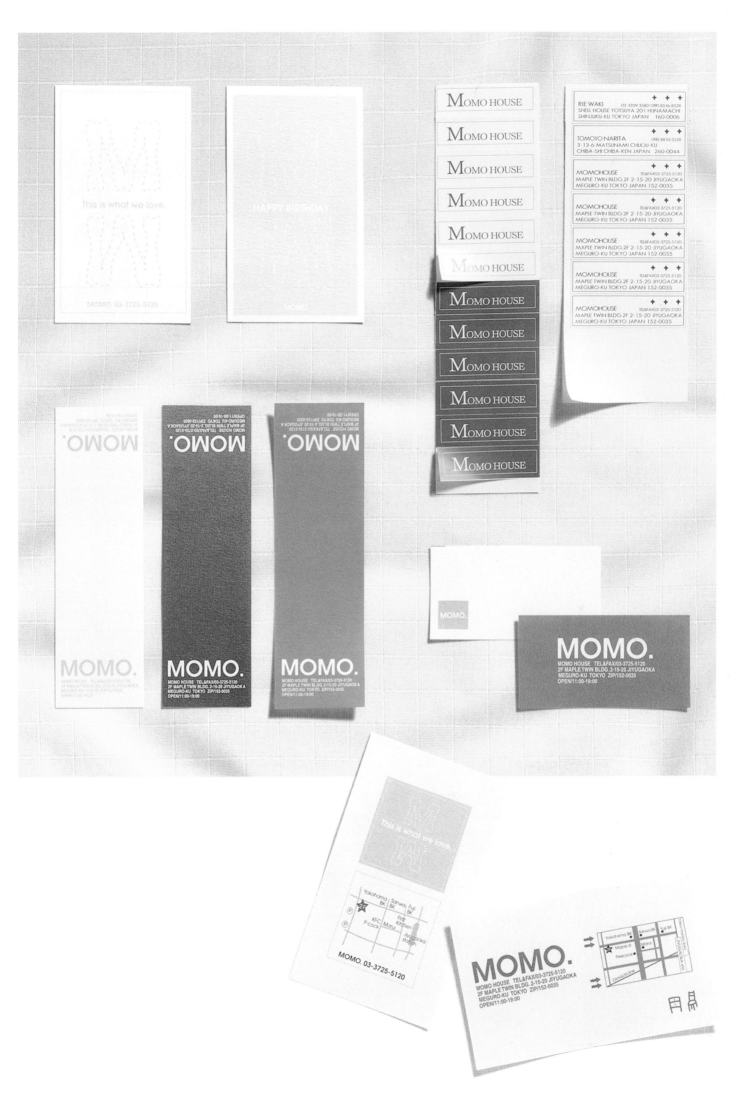

ル・ジャルダン・ドゥ・ジュリアン・エ...ビス
Le jardin de julien & ... bis　Japan
東京都渋谷区恵比寿南1-16-3
1-16-3 Ebisu-minami Shibuya-ku Tokyo

A：立花 巧 Takumi Tachibana
CD, AD：パトリス・ジュリアン Patrice Julien

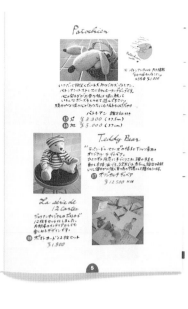

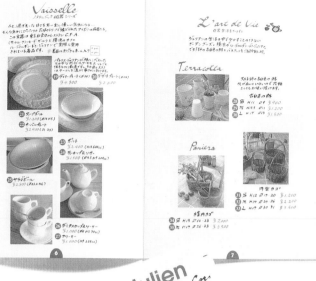

一棟建の中にカフェ、デリ、雑貨を扱うスペースが共存するショップは、ブルターニュ地方の別荘をテーマに、白とブルーで統一したマリンっぽい雰囲気。ロゴは「清涼・清潔感があり、かつウォームデザインである」をコンセプトにデザインされている。

A café, deli, and housewares shop housed under one roof, imaged after a Brittany summer home. The blue and white color scheme creates a marine-like atmosphere. The logo is conceived to be refreshing and clean yet retain a sense of warmth.

カラコ　karako　Japan
東京都目黒区自由が丘1-25-9 セザーム自由が丘ビル
1-25-9 Jiyugaoka Meguro-ku Tokyo

「イースト ミーツ ウエスト」をコンセプトに、食器やインテリア雑貨、アクセサリーなど、生活に関わる品々をアジアをはじめ世界各地から選りすぐり、日本の暮らしに取り入れるスタイルを提案。グラフィックで使用されている桃のイラストもアジア的だ。

Based on the concept "East meets West," the shop proposes making a wide range of items, specially selected from every corner of the world, part of Japanese living. The peach illustration used in the graphics is an Asian rendition.

ノゥティー　naughty　Japan
東京都渋谷区恵比寿南3-2-10 クイーンホームズB1F
B1F Queen Homes, 3-2-10 Ebisu-minami Shibuya-ku Tokyo

A： 石井直子　Naoko Ishii
D： 波多 利結基　Toshiyuki Hata
DF： エルエスアール　LSR

ラベル　Label

スタイリストとして活躍中のオーナーが、世界各地から
買い付けてきた衣料、ファッション小物、家具、インテリア
雑貨等を販売するセレクトショップ。「現在、過去、未来の
融合」をコンセプトにした品ぞろえが魅力的。

Specially selected clothes, fashion accessories, furniture, and
housewares from all corners of the world offered in a shop
owned by a practicing stylist. The dramatically presented
collection of products expresses "the fusion of past, present,
and future."

ギャラリー ビー・ビー・イー　gallery B.B.E.　Japan

東京都豊島区西池袋1-11-1 メトロポリタンプラザ内
Metropolitan Plaza, 1-11-1 Nishi-Ikebukuro Toshima-ku Tokyo

CD, AD：小林良一　Ryoichi Kobayashi
AF, DF：㈱アート プリント ジャパン　Art Print Japan Co., Ltd.

「五感にふれる快適さ」をテーマに、視覚、味覚、嗅覚、聴覚、
触覚に訴えかける製品を提案する雑貨店。グリーン、ブルー、
木成色などのアースカラーをグラフィックに使用すること
により、人間にとっての快適さを表現している。

A variety store offering products based on the theme
"pleasures of the five senses" that appeal to human sight,
sound, touch, taste, and smell. Green, blue, and tan earth
tones in the graphics produce a comforting effect.

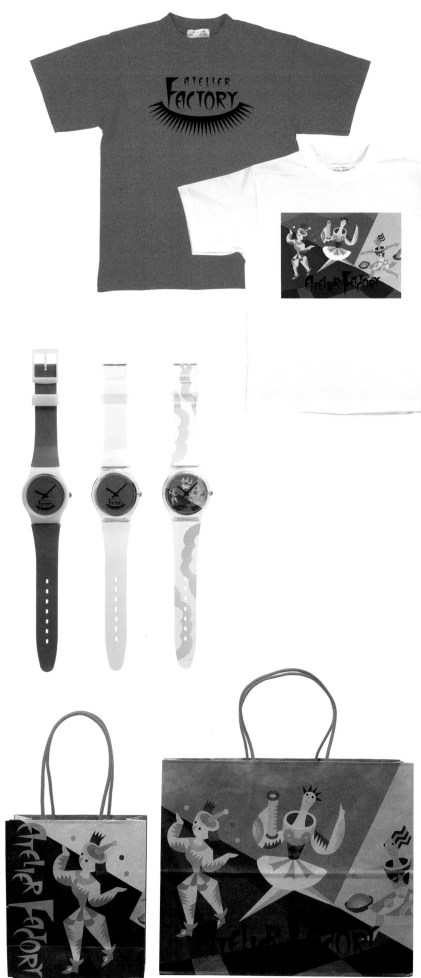

シュウ ウエムラ アトリエファクトリー
shu uemura ATELIER FACTORY　Japan

東京都江東区青海1丁目 パレットタウン ヴィーナスフォート2F
2F Venus Fort, Palette Town, 1 Aomi Koto-ku Tokyo

A：	アンリ・ゲイダン　Henri Gueydan
	金子文子　Fumiko Kaneko
AF：	シィエル・ルージュ・クレアシオン　Ciel Rouge Création
CD, AD：	中塚大輔　Daisuke Nakatsuka
D：	北爪文代　Fumiyo Kitazume
	八木田亮子　Ryoko Yagita
	狩野友子　Tomoko Karino
P：	中村彰三　Shozo Nakamura（1）
I：	藤掛正邦　Masakuni Fujikake
CW：	中塚吐夢　Tom Nakatsuka
	渡辺珍之　Yoshiyuki Watanabe
DF：	㈱中塚大輔広告事務所　Nakatsuka Daisuke Inc.

お台場にある人気のショッピングモール内に誕生した
シュウウエムラの新しいショップは、顧客から口紅など
のオーダーメイドを受け付け、目の前で化粧品を製造す
る「化粧品工場」。グラフィックデザインのイメージは
「懐かしい未来」。

A new Shu Uemura shop debuting in a popular Odaiba mall
where cosmetics are order made before the customer's
eyes — a veritable "cosmetics factory." The graphic design
image is "futuristic nostalgia."

042

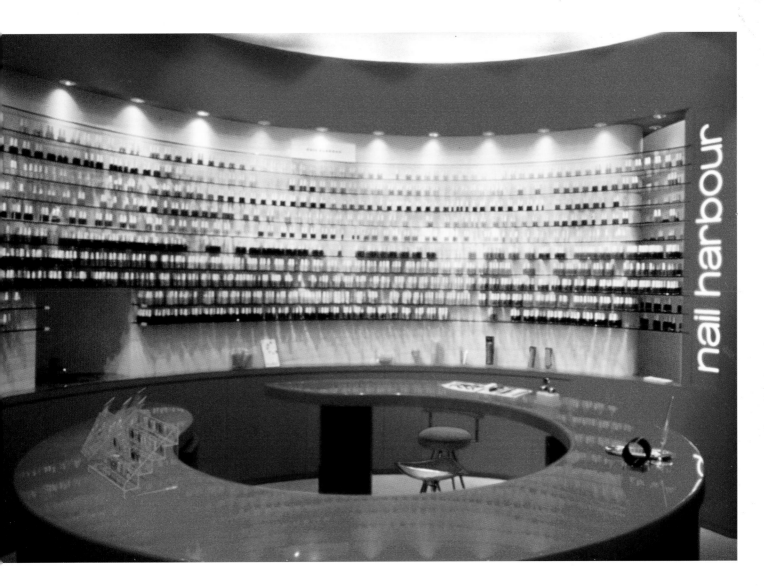

nail harbour

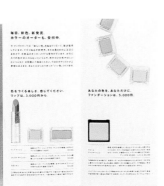

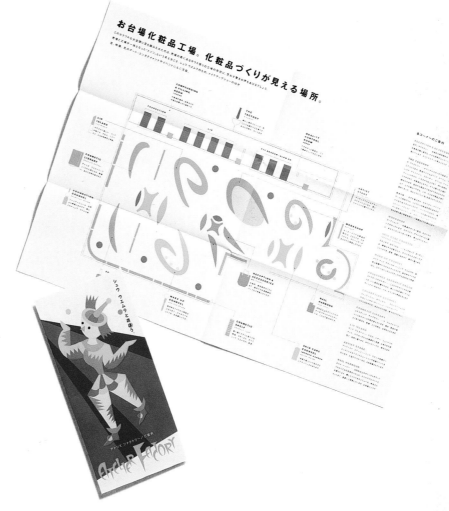

ラッシュ　LUSH　Japan
東京都目黒区自由が丘1-26-8 キクモトビル1F
1F Kikumoto-Bldg., 1-26-8 Jiyugaoka Meguro-ku Tokyo

AF： ㈱ラッシュ ジャパン　Lush Japan Ltd.
　　 ㈱乃村工藝社　Nomura Co., Ltd.

フリーペーパー　PR Magazine

手作りの新鮮な化粧品や石けんを、ヨーロッパにある
デリカテッセンやチーズ屋のような量り売りスタイル
で提供する店。黒板に大きく書かれた商品名や用途、木
箱に積み上げられた商品など、まるで食品売り場のよ
うなディスプレイが視覚的な効果を上げている。

Fresh, handmade toiletries and soap sold by weight
European delicatessen/cheese shop style. Product names
and uses handwritten on blackboards, products packed in
wood crates — food market-like displays create a visually
appealing store atmosphere.

サプリメント ヤ（サプ） Sup. Supplement-Ya Japan

東京都新宿区新宿3-24-3 ALTA B2F
B2F ALTA, 3-24-3 Shinjuku Shinjuku-ku Tokyo

AF： ㈱ノバ・コーポレーション Nova Corporation
Planner, CD： 坪田恭吾　Kyogo Tsubota
AD： 大川栄司　Eiji Okawa
D： 阿部 均　Hitoshi Abe
P： 赤尾昌則　Masanori Akao
CW： 松尾千鶴子　Chizuko Matsuo
DF： ㈱ケイ・クリエイティブ・ファクトリー　K-Creative Factory Co., Ltd.

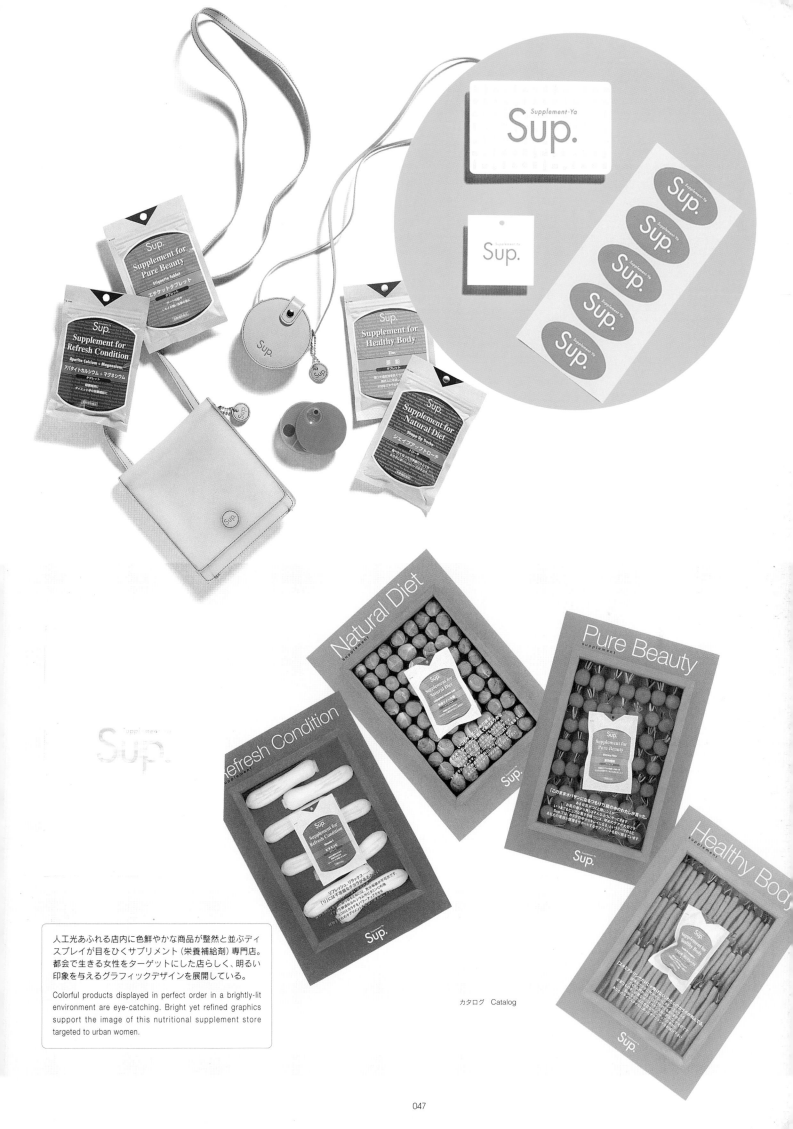

人工光あふれる店内に色鮮やかな商品が整然と並ぶディスプレイが目をひくサプリメント（栄養補給剤）専門店。都会で生きる女性をターゲットにした店らしく、明るい印象を与えるグラフィックデザインを展開している。

Colorful products displayed in perfect order in a brightly-lit environment are eye-catching. Bright yet refined graphics support the image of this nutritional supplement store targeted to urban women.

カタログ　Catalog

International Beauty and Healthcare

ブーツ Boots Japan

東京都中央区銀座5-4-3 対鶴館ビル1-2F
1-2F Taikakukan-Bldg., 5-4-3 Ginza Chuo-ku Tokyo

A： 小野 浩 Hiroshi Ono
AF： ㈱丹青社 Tanseisha Co., Ltd.
CD： 嶋崎政樹 Masaki Shimazaki
千葉告理子 Noriko Chiba (1)
AD, D： 村田 聡 Satoshi Murata
DF： マッキャンエリクソン McCann-Erickson
オフィス コクリコ Office Coqulicot (1)

1 レシート Receipt

化粧品、医薬品等を販売するイギリス生まれのショップ。
女性を内側と外側から美しくする情報を発信するという
コンセプトのもと、白と青を基調としてデザインされた
店舗は、様々な色彩があふれるショッピング街において、
効果を発揮している。

An English cosmetics and drug store chain offering
information and products to make women beautiful inside
and out hits Japan. The basic blue and white store design
demonstrates its effectiveness when seen in colorful
shopping districts.

グリーンレーベル リラクシング
Green Label RELAXING Japan
東京都新宿区新宿3-38-2 ルミネ新宿2 2F
2F Lumine Shinjuku-2, 3-38-2 Shinjuku Shinjuku-ku Tokyo

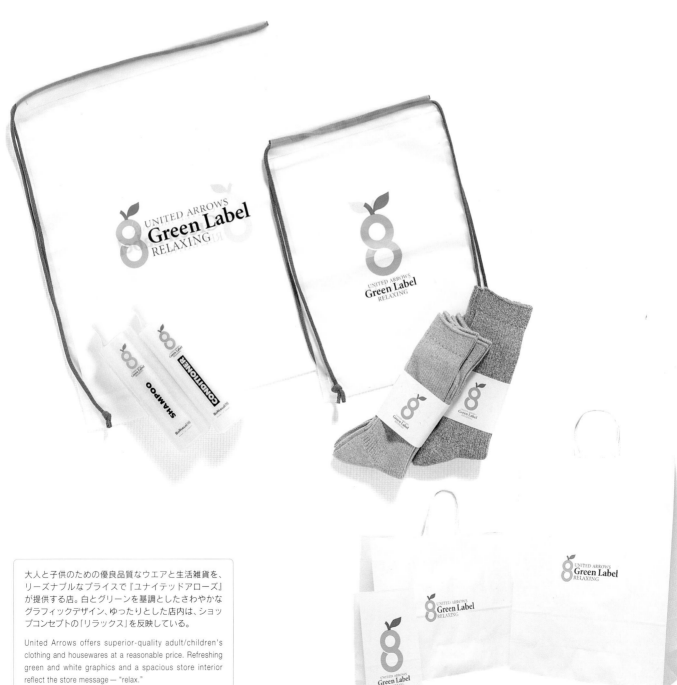

大人と子供のための優良品質なウエアと生活雑貨を、
リーズナブルなプライスで『ユナイテッドアローズ』
が提供する店。白とグリーンを基調としたさわやかな
グラフィックデザイン、ゆったりとした店内は、ショッ
プコンセプトの「リラックス」を反映している。

United Arrows offers superior-quality adult/children's
clothing and housewares at a reasonable price. Refreshing
green and white graphics and a spacious store interior
reflect the store message — "relax."

インディヴィ ライフ　INDIVI LIFE　Japan
東京都港区南青山5-11-8
5-11-8 Minami-Aoyama Minato-ku Tokyo

A : 真保 毅　Takeshi Shinbo
AF : 真保デザイン事務所　Shinbo Design Office
CD, D : 田山淳朗　Atsuro Tayama
AD : 八木 保　Tamotsu Yagi

「世界中のいいもの」をキーワードに集めた雑貨を販売するスペースとカフェをブティックに併設した、アパレルブランドがプロデュースする複合店。ブランドイメージの白黒の配色と雑貨の形をデザイン化したアイコンを、この店専用のグラフィックツールに使用している。

A combination boutique/café produced by an apparel brand offering a selection of household goods that meet the criteria, "good things from around the world." The black and white color scheme and pictographs depicting various household products form the store's distinctive graphic vocabulary.

050

マーガレット・ハウエル ライフスタイルショップ 神南
Margaret Howell Lifestyle Shop Jinnan Japan

東京都渋谷区神南1-13-8 パークアヴェニュー神南1F
1F Park Avenue Jinnan, 1-13-8 Jinnan Shibuya-ku Tokyo

CD： マーガレット・ハウエル　Margaret Howell (3)
AD： ステファニー・ナッシュ　Stephanie Nash (3)
D： マーガレット・ハウエル　Margaret Howell (1,2)
D： アンソニー・ナッシュ　Anthony Nash (3)
P： マーガレット・ハウエル　Margaret Howell (2)
P： コト・ボロフォ　Koto Bolofo (3)
Stylist： ヴェネシア・スコット　Venetia Scott (3)
DF： マイケル・ナッシュ・アソシエイツ
　　　Micheal Nash Associates (3)

2　メニュー　Menu

2　招待状　Invitation Card

3　カタログ　Catalog

マーガレット・ハウエルが生活全般にわたるそのセンス
で、プロデュースした衣食住のトータルショップ。店内
の商品はもとより、グラフィック、家具、食品など、あら
ゆる物を彼女自身がこのショップのためにデザインし、
買い付けている。

A "total living" shop based on Margaret Howell's sensibilities
as applied to the multi-dimensions of living. Ms. Howell
designs and/or procures the graphics, furniture, foods, and
a variety of other items for the shop on an on-going basis, let
alone the products.

クリーニング ストア CLeaninG store Japan

東京都渋谷区神宮前6-19-20
6-19-20 Jingumae Shibuya-ku Tokyo

AF：㈲スタジオ グレイプ Studio Grape Inc.

cleaning
100%

cleaning store
6-19-20 Jingumae shibuya-ku Tokyo phone 03-3797-7633
open / weekday 11:00-20:00 / weekend.national holidays 10:30-20:00

Café
cleaning

phone 03-3797-5707
open / weekday 9:00-22:30 / weekend.national holidays 10:30-22:00

ブティックにカフェが併設された、新しい形の複合ショップ。「スマイル＝コミュニケーション」をコンセプトに、顧客にとって身近な存在でありつつも、これからの時代性を提案していく"ストア"を目指している。

The unique name and logo of this new-style combination boutique/café imbue it with personality. Based on the concept "a smile=communication," the store strives to be one that customers perceive as a familiar entity, while offering a glimpse of times to come.

cLeaning	TAILLE
EXTERIEUR : 100% CASUAL INTERIEUR : 100% CONFORT	1 u n
ATTENTION	

-épuration de l'esprit
-relaxation
-équilibre
-simplicité et intelligence
vêtements 100%confortables

 ラベル Label

cLeaning
SOURIRE ET COMMUNICATION
-épuration et l'esprit
-relaxation
-équilibre
-simplité et intelligence
-vêtemets 100% confortables

キャスロン　caslon　Japan

宮城県仙台市泉区紫山1-1-4 泉パークタウン紫山
Izumi Park Town Murasakiyama, 1-1-4 Murasakiyama Izumi-ku
Sendai-shi Miyagi

A : 原 成光　Shigemitsu Hara
AF : ジョイントセンター㈱　Joint Center Inc.
CD : 宮田 識　Satoru Miyata
AD, D : 渡邊良重 Yoshie Watanabe / 植原亮輔　Ryosuke Uehara
DF : ディー・ブロス㈱ドラフト）D-Bros（Draft Co., Ltd.）

パンの製造・販売を中心とした複合ショップ。天然酵母のこ
だわりパン、香りのよい紅茶などが楽しめる、光あふれる気
持ちのいいカフェスペース、そしてお皿やカップなど上質の
テーブル雑貨が並ぶプロダクトショップで構成されている。

A combination shop centered on the production/sales of fresh-
baked bread. The shop is composed of a light-filled café space
where customers can enjoy naturally leavened breads and
fragrant teas, and a retail space offering cups, dishes and other
fine tableware.

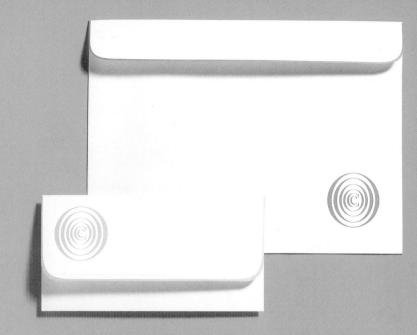

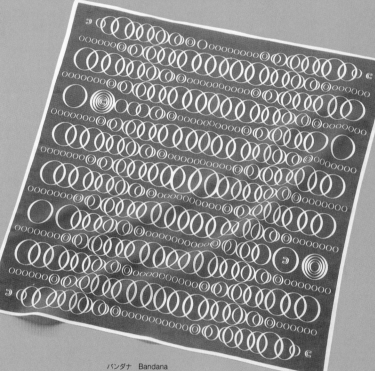

バンダナ　Bandana

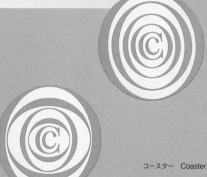

コースター　Coaster

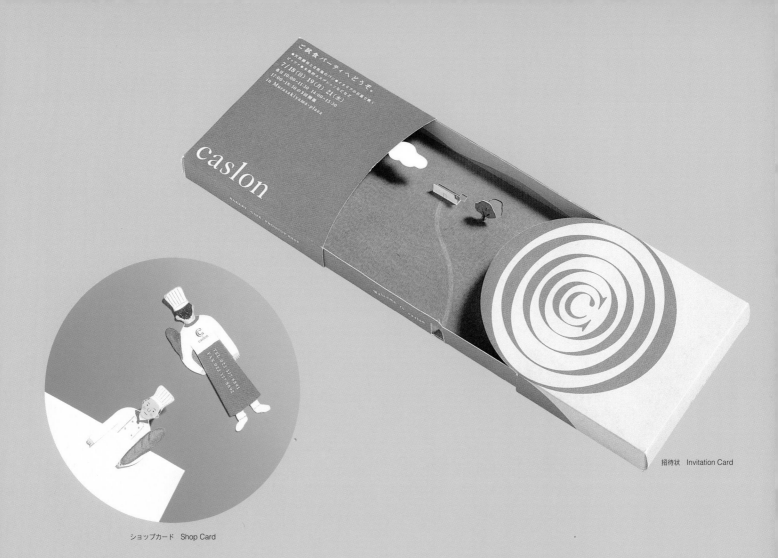

招待状　Invitation Card

ショップカード　Shop Card

ポストカード　Post Card

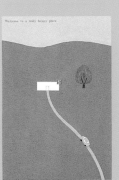

北川村「モネの庭」マルモッタン
Jardin de Monet Marmottan au Village de Kitagawa　Japan

高知県安芸郡北川村野友甲1100
1100 Ko Notomo Kitagawa-mura Aki-gun Kochi

　　A：尾坂昇治　Shoji Osaka
　　AF：㈱シナジー　Synergy Co., Ltd.
AD, D：八馬 未包子　Mihoko Hachiuma
　　CW：久保理子　Masako Kubo
　　DF：フリーラ　Free·la

モネの庭園と邸宅を再現した公園の中にある土産店とレストラン。モネに出会う小さな旅をイメージし、土産店で使用する包装紙も、フランスへ旅したような非日常的感覚を味わえる演出効果を狙ってデザインされている。

A restaurant and gift shop in a park recreating Monet's home and garden. Based on an imaginary journey to the world of Monet, the entire space (down to the wrapping paper used in the gift shop) is staged to give customers the exotic sense of having traveled to France.

トリコ trico Japan

東京都渋谷区神宮前6-9-1 B1F
B1F, 6-9-1 Jingumae Shibuya-ku Tokyo

CD： 佐伯 仁 Hitoshi Saeki (2)
AD, D： 佐藤益大 Masuhiro Sato (2)
D： 桜井敦子 Atsuko Sakurai (3)
D： 佐伯 仁 Hitoshi Saeki (1)
P： 佐伯 仁 Hitoshi Saeki (2)
I： 桜井敦子 Atsuko Sakurai (2)
AF, DF： エア コンディションド Air Conditioned

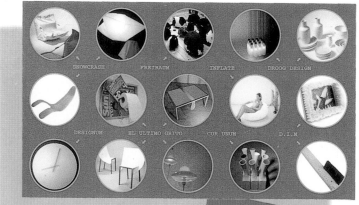

1 ショップカード Shop Card

1 会員証 Member's Card

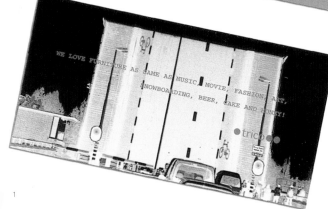

1

1

独自の視点で集められた家具とインテリア雑貨を販売するこの店のコンセプトは、「DESIGN AGAINST TREND（流行から解放されたデザイン）」。商品カタログを兼ねている『TRICO DESIGN BOOK』のデザインと編集にもそのこだわりが見える。

"Design against trend" is the concept behind this attention-getting store offering a unique collection of furniture and housewares. The same approach is seen in the design and editing of their "Trico Design Book," which doubles as a product catalog.

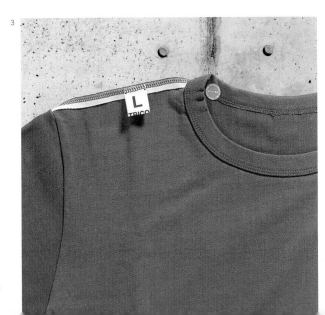

九印雑貨店　Cue-Brand V. S.　Japan

東京都武蔵野市吉祥寺南町1-6-5-12
1-6-5-12 Kichijoji Minami-machi Musashino-shi Tokyo

A：中村友昭　Tomoaki Nakamura

タグ　Tag

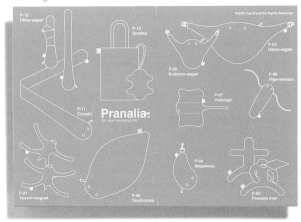

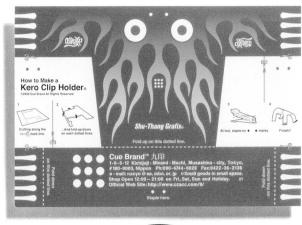

「進化」をテーマに夫婦で雑貨を製作。伝統的なモチーフや、
生物の形態・機能などに注目し、独特の視点で新しい雑貨
を生み出している。初の直営店は、高架下の猥雑な空間に
ポッカリと出現した謎の「雑貨版キオスク」のイメージ。

A new approach to sundries based on the theme "evolution"
with attention paid to traditional motifs and organic forms and
functions produced by a couple with an unique viewpoint.
Their first retail store stands out as a curious "sundries kiosk"
in a seedy space under an overpass.

ヴァキューム・レコーズ　vacuum records　Japan
東京都渋谷区神宮前3-22-1 神宮前スクエア201
201, 3-22-1 Jingumae Shibuya-ku Tokyo

A： 西堀 晋　Shin Nishibori
AF： シン プロダクツ　Shin Products
DF： ヴァキューム・レコーズ　Vacuum Records, Inc.

ポストカード　Post Card

大阪に続いてファッションの街、原宿にオープンしたオリジナルレコードプレーヤーとオモチャを扱う店。京都にある話題のカフェ『efish』の設計者、西堀 晋がデザインを手掛けた店内は、従来のオモチャ屋のイメージを払拭。おしゃれな空間となっている。

The Harajuku fashion district branch of an Osaka record player and toy store. Designer Shin Nishibori (famed for the Kyoto café "efish") eradicates the conventional toy store image with his stylish interior.

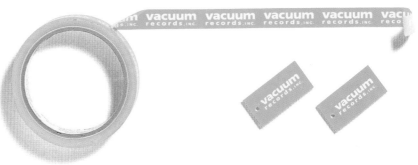

エロティック　EROTIC　Japan
東京都渋谷区神南1-20-1-2F
2F, 1-20-1 Jinnan Shibuya-ku Tokyo

P： 五十嵐 真　Shin Igarashi (1)
　　田辺わかな　Wakana Tanabe (2)
　　エロティック デザイン ワークス　Erotic Design Works (3)
DF： エロティック デザイン ワークス　Erotic Design Works

ポストカード　Post Card

2 リーフレット
Leaflet

柔らかな発想から誕生した、オリジナルデザインの家具、家電、インテリア製品を販売する店。「エロティック」という店内からは想像できない、ポップでカラフルなアイテムが店内にあふれている。

A store offering originally designed furniture, small appliances and housewares born of flexible thinking. In contrast to the image the name "Erotic" might inspire, the open store interior is brimming with colorful items.

エフィッシュ　efish　Japan
京都府京都市下京区木屋町通五条下ル西橋詰町798-1
798-1 Nishi-Hashizume-cho Gojosagaru Kiyamachidori
Shimogyo-ku Kyoto-shi Kyoto

A： 西堀 晋　Shin Nishibori
AF： シン プロダクツ　Shin Products
D, I： 近藤朋幸　Tomoyuki Kondo
P： 高山幸三　Kozo Takayama / 西堀 晋　Shin Nishibori (1)
CW： 西堀 晋　Shin Nishibori

1　ポストカード
Post Card

かつて遊廓があった場所に出現した、オリジナル雑貨も
販売しているカフェ。その昔、この場所で遊女のサイン
として使用されていた「金魚」を、店内やグラフィックに
あしらっている。夜、川の対岸から見る店内は、ほんやり
と闇夜に浮かぶ水槽のようで美しい。

A café selling original interior goods in a former red-light
district. Goldfish, once used in the area as signs by ladies of
the night, accent the interior and graphics. Seen at night
from the other side of the river, the café has the charm of a
fish bowl glowing faintly in the dark.

コンシェルジュ　CONCIERGE　Japan
東京都渋谷区猿楽町10-14 代官山パシフィック1F
1F Daikanyama Pacific, 10-14 Sarugaku-cho Shibuya-ku Tokyo

CD, AD： 神谷敬久　Takahisa Kamiya
　　DF： ㈱スーパー プランニング　Super Planning Co., Ltd.

旅をテーマにした雑貨を取り扱うセレクトショップ。デザイン性や感性を重視して集められた商品と、店内ディスプレイのイメージコントロールにより、まさしく旅における「コンシェルジュ」の役割を果たす店づくりを目指している。

A specialty shop offering sundries based on the theme "journey." A collection of products that reflect design sensibility and sensitivity, and design-controlled display help create a store that performs the role a concierge plays on a journey.

メイド・オン・アース
MADE ON EARTH USA

12188 Ventura Blvd., Studio City, CA 91604

CD： マルゴ・ナハス　Margo Nahas
AD, D： ジェイ・ビゴン　Jay Vigon
P： アラン・シェーファー　Alan Shaffer
I： キャロリン・プラセンシア　Caroline Plasencia

ステッカー　Sticker

ポストカード　Post Card

キャラクター、ロゴ、ギフト商品、衣類、家具の全てはロサンゼルス
のデザイナー、ジェイ・ビゴンによる創造。カリフォルニアのスタ
ジオシティにある『メイド・オン・アース』は、ビゴンの非常に個性
的なスタイルによる新しいイメージのデザインであふれている。

Characters, logos, gift merchandise, clothing and furniture, all created
by Los Angeles designer, Jay Vigon. Made On Earth, located in Studio
City, California, features many applications of new images in Vigon's
very individual style.

ポップチューン トーキョー
POPTUNE TOKYO　Japan
東京都渋谷区猿楽町12-8
12-8 Sarugaku-cho Shibuya-ku Tokyo

CD, AD：神谷敬久　Takahisa Kamiya
DF：㈱スーパー プランニング
　　　Super Planning Co., Ltd.

東京ニューレトロをキーワードに、60'S、70'Sの東京スタ
イルに現在のクオリティをプラスした生活スタイルを、若
い女性に提案する店。新しいけれどどこか懐かしい感じが
する、インテリア雑貨とファッション雑貨を扱っている。

A collection of interior and fashion accessories both new and
somehow nostalgic. A store offering young girls a style of living
called "Tokyo New Retro" — 60s and 70s Tokyo style with an
added contemporary quality.

ミスター フレンドリー デイリー ストア
MR. FRIENDLY DAILY STORE   Japan
東京都渋谷区恵比寿西2-18-6 SPビル1F
1F SP-Bldg., 2-18-6 Ebisu-nishi Shibuya-ku Tokyo

CD, AD： 神谷敬久 Takahisa Kamiya
    DF： ㈱スーパー プランニング Super Planning Co., Ltd.

文具雑貨とオリジナル菓子を扱う複合ショップで、「フレ
ンドリー」をキーワードとしたコミュニケーションスペ
ースをつくりあげている。ロゴに使用されているのは
「Mr. Friendly」という名のオリジナルキャラクター。

"Friendly" is the keyword behind this combination
stationery/confectionery shop designed to encourage
communications. The logo includes the original cartoon
character, Mr. Friendly.

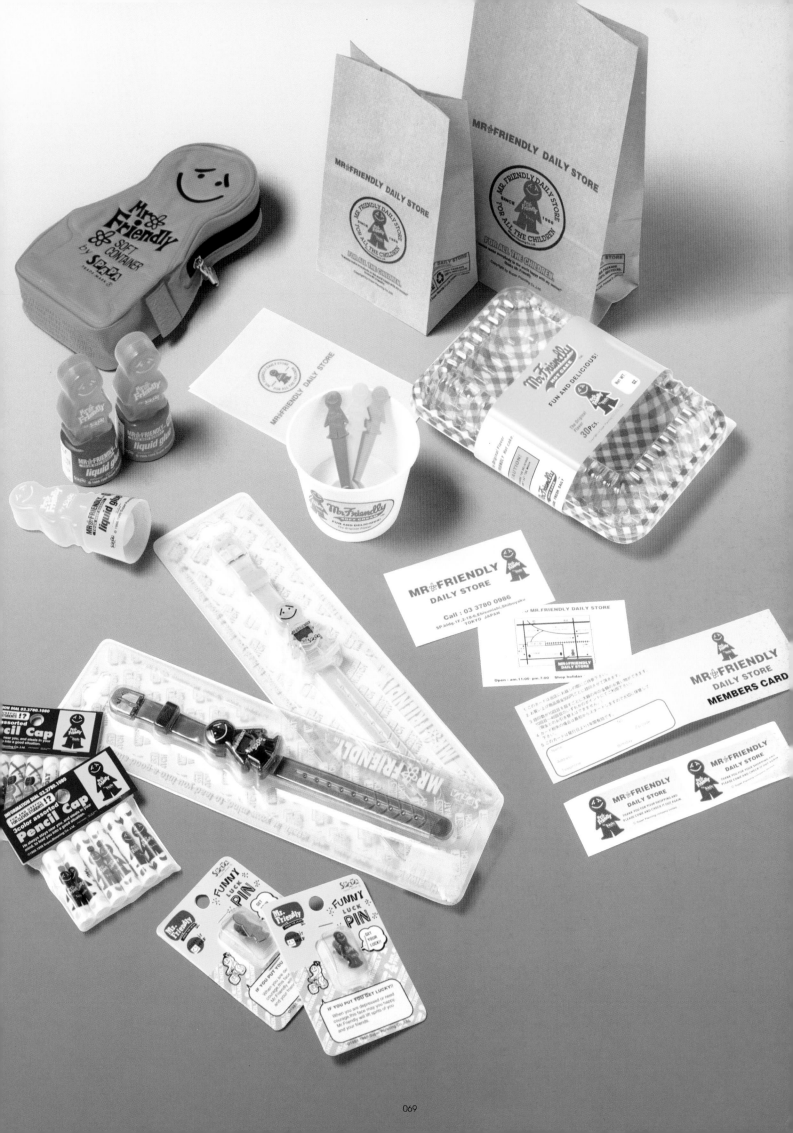

書泉ブックドーム　SHOSEN BOOK DOME　Japan
埼玉県川口市栄町3-4-3
3-4-3 Sakae-cho Kawaguchi-shi Saitama

A： 鈴木伸之　Nobuyuki Suzuki
AF： ㈱鈴木アソシエイツ　N. Suzuki & Associates
CD, AD, D, I： 長谷川光宏　Mitsuhiro Hasegawa

しおり、ギフト用包装紙、ショッピングバッグ等のグラフィックツールを、顧客が本に親しみ楽しんで購入してもらえるよう、温かいイメージで展開。店内は機能性を最優先させたつくりになっている。

Graphic applications — bookmarks, wrapping paper, shopping bags — express the warmth this bookstore hopes customers will feel as they become intimate with and enjoy books. The store interior puts priority on function; the orthodox image is in line with conventional Japanese bookstores.

ブックス ルー・エ BOOKS RUHE Japan

東京都武蔵野市吉祥寺本町1-14-3
1-14-3 Honcho Kichijoji Musashino-shi Tokyo

D, I: キン シオタニ Kin Shiotani

ポストカード Post Card

一度は住んでみたい街として東京の若者から支持されている「吉祥寺」という街に合わせて、書店をまず人が集まる場所として考え、店舗の設計がなされている。白のイメージで統一された店内は、まるでブティックのような清潔感にあふれている。

A bookstore designed to be a gathering spot to match its Kichijoji locale, an area of Tokyo often cited by young people as a desirable place to live. The unified white interior space has the feeling of a boutique.

ゴシック ラウンジ カフェ
Gothic Lounge Café　Japan
東京都渋谷区神宮前1-2-13
1-2-13 Jingumae Shibuya-ku Tokyo

A, CD, AD, D：アマール・ゲソウス　Amal Guessous

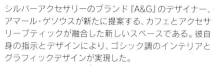

シルバーアクセサリーのブランド『A&G』のデザイナー、アマール・ゲソウスが新たに提案する、カフェとアクセサリーブティックが融合した新しいスペースである。彼自身の指示とデザインにより、ゴシック調のインテリアとグラフィックデザインが実現した。

Amal Guessous, designer of the silver-accessories brand A&G, merges a café and accessories boutique, offering a new kind of retail space. The distinctive Gothic-style interior and graphics were also designed and directed by Mr. Guessous.

NU

DRINK

FFEE／ホットコーヒー	¥500
／エスプレッソ	¥500
PRESSO／ダブルエスプレッソ	¥650
ATE／ホットチョコレート	¥600
NO／ホットカプチーノ	¥600
／ホットカフェラテ	¥600
ホットカフェモカ	¥650
ティー（ダージリン）	¥600
	各¥600

ズヒップ＆ハイビスカス

CAFFAINATED
ARGE)

かかりません。）

ICED DRINK

ICED COFFEE／アイスコーヒー	¥550
ICED CAPPUCCINO／アイスカプチーノ	¥650
ICED CAFE LATTE／アイスカフェラテ	¥650
ICED CAFE MOCHA／アイスカフェモカ	¥700
ICED TEA／アイスティー	¥650
JUICE／ジュース	各¥600

＊ ORANGE JUICE／オレンジジュース

＊ GRAPEFRUIT JUICE／グレープフルーツジュース

SPRING WATER (PANNA) ／スプリングウオーター（パンナ）	¥500
SPARKLING WATER (PERRIER) ／スパークリングウオーター（ペリエ）	¥500

SWEETS

COOKIE／クッキー	各¥200

TOKYO   LOS ANGELES

Gothic Lounge Cafe

JINGUMAE-YACHIYO BLD. 1-2-13, JINGUMAE,
SHIBUYA-KU, TOKYO, 150-0001 JAPAN.
PH/FX 03-5775-2725

ステッカー　Sticker

レ・ピアフス　Les Piafs USA

2118 Second Avenue, Seattle, WA 98121

CD, AD： パトリシア・ベリーア　Patricia Belyea
　　　D： ケリー・ルイス　Kelli Lewis
　　　P： ロジャー・シェイバー　Roger Scheiber
　　　DF： ベリーア　Belyea

ステッカー　Sticker

ステッカー　Sticker

ショップカード　Shop Card

ヴィンテージ・リビングとフレンチ・カントリー・スタイルとい
う店のコンセプトを視覚化するために、春、夏、秋、冬、フレン
チ・カントリー、エレガンスを基調テーマとして6つの異なるコ
ラージュが製作された。それらのコラージュは、DMの葉書、値札、
名刺それぞれの裏側、またショッピングバッグに施されている。

Incorporating the store's concept of vintage living and French country
style, six different collages were created based respectively on the
themes fall, winter, summer, spring, French country, and elegance.
The images are applied to the backs of the direct-mail postcards,
price tags, business cards and shopping bags.

ジー・エイチ・バス＆コー
G. H. Bass & Co. USA

D： ジム・ブラウン　Jim Brown
　　ポーラ・シェア　Paula Scher
　　リサ・マツァール　Lisa Mazur
DF： ペンタグラム　Pentagram

無作為に収集された古いグラフィックスや広告またパッケージが
再解釈され、ニューイングランドの大いなる遺産を引き継ぐブラン
ドのイメージに添って、秩序だって整理されている。マークはブラン
ドの最も有名な商品「ウィージン・モカシン」から引用されており、
このモカシンの作り方はアメリカ先住民のカヌーからきている。

An old, disorderly collection of graphics, advertising and packaging is
reinterpreted as a coordinated system of imagery that celebrates the
brand's strong New England heritage. The identifying icon refers to the
brand's most famous product, the Weejun moccasin, the construction
of which was derived from the Native-American canoe.

ミハエル・ネグリン オリジナル デザインズ
MICHAL NEGRIN ORIGINAL DESIGNS Japan
東京都江東区青海1丁目 パレットタウン ヴィーナスフォート2F
2F Venus Fort, Palette Town, 1 Aomi Koto-ku Tokyo

Planner, CD, AD : ロン・ヤハブ・バルーフ Ron Yahav Baruch
　　　　A, D : 宮田愛美 Megumi Miyata
　　　　　 D : ミハエル・ネグリン Michal Negrin
　　　　D, P : ダナ・サデー Dana Sadeh (1)
　　　　　 I : ジェニア・テトリンコ Jenia Tetrinco
　　　AF, DF : ㈱ヌルハウス Null Haus

1 カタログ Catalog

ポストカード Post Card

新鮮な色使いとノスタルジックな商品デザインで注目され
るジュエリーショップ。ラブ、ロマンス、ビューティ、フリ
ーダムから成る4つのテーマを融合させて表現したドラマ
ティックな空間演出も女性のハートをとらえている。

A jewelry shop known for its nostalgic product design with a fresh
use of color. The dramatic retail space expressing the fusion of
four themes — love, romance, beauty, and freedom — has swept
the female heart.

ガブリエレ・クレーシュマー
GABRIELE KRÄTSCHMER Germany
Friedrichst. 10, Wiesbaden 65185

CD, AD, D： オリバー・ウェイラー Oliver Weiller
　　　　　 ニーナ・ラップ Nina Rapp
　　　 P： フランク・カイサール Frank Kayser
　　 CW： クラウディア・ハード Claudia Herdt
　　 DF： ウェイラー＆ラップ デザイン Weiller & Rapp Design

『ガブリエレ・クレーシュマー』は一店舗内で幅広い美容商品を詰め合せ提供している。香水と化粧品は彼女が全世界から見つけてきた手に入れにくい商品。また全商品はカタログからメールオーダー、及びインターネット上で購入可能である。

Gabriele Krätschmer brings together a broad assortment of beauty products in one shop. Perfumes and cosmetics rarely found elsewhere are among the range of products she searches the world over to find. All products are presented in a catalog and sold via mail-order and/or the internet.

シンジ S·H·I·N·J·I Japan
東京都港区南青山5-4-24
5-4-24 Minami-Aoyama Minato-ku Tokyo

A： 高橋紀人 Norito Takahashi
AF： ㈱エグジット メタル ワーク サプライ
　　Exit Metal Work Supply
CD： 直井新治 Shinji Naoi
AD, D： 直井真知子 Machiko Naoi
D： 相原直人 Naoto Aihara (1)
P： 輿 英治 Eiji Koshi (1)
I： 杉本昌雄 Masao Sugimoto (1)
CW： 直井真知子 Machiko Naoi (1)

アルミ材とガラスで構成した、ギャラリー風の無機質な
空間が印象的なジュエリーショップ。商品はシンプル＆
モダンなフォルムながら、どこか温かみが感じられるデ
ザイン。その雰囲気を壊さないよう、透明感のあるパッケ
ージを展開している。

Inorganic aluminum and glass form an impressive gallery-like
jewelry shop. Transparent packaging enhances the jewelry,
designed to be sharp and modern yet embody a touch of warmth.

1 ポストカード Post Card

ポーカー フェイス　POKER FACE　Japan

東京都渋谷区宇田川町41-26 為田ビル1F
1F Tameda-Bldg., 41-26 Udagawa-cho Shibuya-ku Tokyo

A：内田 繁　Shigeru Uchida
AF：㈱スタジオ80　Studio 80
AD：清水昭宏　Akihiro Shimizu (3)
LD：野間義剛　Yoshitake Noma
D：加藤幸男　Yukio Kato (2)
D：野間義剛　Yoshitake Noma (1)
P：佐藤正治　Shoji Sato (3)
DF：㈱ガリバー計画　Gulliver Keikaku Co., Ltd. (3)
　　スピーパーグラフィックス　Speeper Graphics (2)
　　野間デザイン室　Noma Design Office (1)

ショップカード　Shop Card

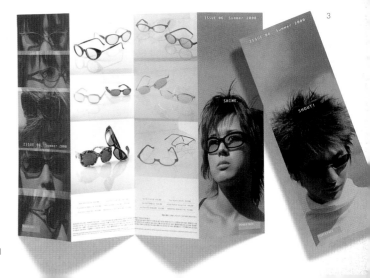

デザイン性と機能性をあわせ持つ、スタイルのある眼鏡フレームおよびその未来形を提案する眼鏡店。クリアで無機質な空間とグラフィックデザインは近未来的な雰囲気を漂わせている。

An optical shop offering stylish eyeglass frames that balance form and function, along with a glimpse at the future of the art. The clear, inorganic space and graphics instill a contemporary/futuristic atmosphere.

フォーナインズ　999.9　Japan

東京都渋谷区神南1-20-8 芳賀電ビル1-2F
1-2F Hagaden-Bldg., 1-20-8 Jinnan Shibuya-ku Tokyo

AF, CD： フォーナインズ プロジェクト　Four Nines Project
　　CD： 土居輝彦　Teruhiko Doi (1)
AD, D： 若山トシオ　Toshio Wakayama (1)
　　P： 中川正子　Masako Nakagawa (1)
　　　　井置 修　Osamu Ioki (1)
　　DF： 若山デザインオフィス　Wakayama Design Office (1)

店の主役であるメガネの存在を中心に考えたショップデザインが魅力的。視力矯正器具としてのメガネの機能性を追求して生まれた商品の美しいフォルムとイメージを、グラフィックにもおとしこんでいる。

An attractive store designed to give the principle product — eyeglasses — the spotlight. The beautiful form and image that the function of eyeglasses as vision correction equipment gives rise to manifests in the graphics as well.

ジー ビー ガファス　G. B. Gafas　Japan

大阪府大阪市中央区南船場4-8-5 南船場大阪産業ビル1F
1F Minami Senba Osaka Sangyo-Bldg., 4-8-5 Minami-Senba
Chuo-ku Osaka-shi Osaka

D, I: 千秋育子　Yasuko Senshu（1）

1　ショップカード　Shop Card

リーフレット　Leaflet

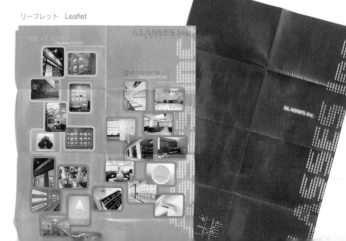

クラシックを基調としながらも、明るくポップな店内の
イメージをグラフィックツールにも反映。しかし眼鏡ケー
スやクロスは使いやすさを重視し、あえてシンプルな
デザインにしている。

With an underlying classic tone, the graphics reflect the pop
image of the store interior. Simple design simultaneously
emphasizes the importance placed on ease of use of
eyeglass cases and cloths.

へム HeM Japan

東京都渋谷区代官山町10-1 りーぶる代官山
Libre Daikanyama, 10-1 Daikanyama-cho
Shibuya-ku Tokyo

AF： ㈱シーピーシー CPC Inc.
A： 山崎一哉 Kazuya Yamasaki
LD： マーカス・キールテン Markus Kiersztan
D： 布袋真紀子 Makiko Hotei

ラベル Label

機能的なフォルムのバッグをビビッドな色目で提案する
ショップ。ロゴは、『ナイキ』のアートディレクションを
手掛けていたマーカス・キールテン氏が制作。グラフィッ
クデザインにはバウハウスの構成主義的なテイストが加
えられている。

A shop offering handbags in functional forms and vivid
colors. Nike art director Markus Kiersztan designed the logo;
the graphics reflect a touch of Bauhaus-style Constructivism.

サック SAC Japan

東京都渋谷区神宮前4-4-8
4-4-8 Jingumae Shibuya-ku Tokyo

CD：吉尾良里 Rari Yoshio
D：細沼利奈子 Rinako Hosonuma
Decorator：松尾 泉 Izumi Matsuo
妻嶋孝夫 Takao Tsumashima

人と人のコミュニケーションから生まれる商品づくり。豊富なアイテムとバリエーションを持つバッグや小物雑貨たち。顧客に「何かありそう」とワクワクさせるこの店の空間演出とグラフィックデザインは、楽しいムードにあふれている。

A variety store with a rich range of handbags and accessories developed through the process of person-to-person communications. Interior design and graphics create a fun mood, one that excites customers with the anticipation of "finding that something."

SAC

We love creating as long as we have the passion
we want to continue to work

'00-01: SAC
Autumn/Winter
Collection

SAC

SAC BYS
Hi Brids

SAC GIRLS
New Wave

CHÉROSITA
New Standard

SAC

SAC GIRLS   New Millennium
● Acoustic Gear
● Classical Sweet

SAC BYS   Feel The Light
● Zest
● Nifty

CHÉROSITA   New Luxe
● Glamorous
● Luxe
● Standard

Millennium

2000 SAC SPRING/SUMMER
COLLECTION

ポストカード   Post Card

MILLENNIUM WINTER
SALE

SAC

SHOP OPEN.
1999 September 29th(wed)
MATSUYA GINZA

ブール ヘア アンド メイクアップ
POOL hair and make-up　Japan
東京都渋谷区神宮前1-20-13 ノーサレンダーB1F
B1F, 1-20-13 Jingumae Shibuya-ku Tokyo

AD, D：波多 利結基　Toshiyuki Hata

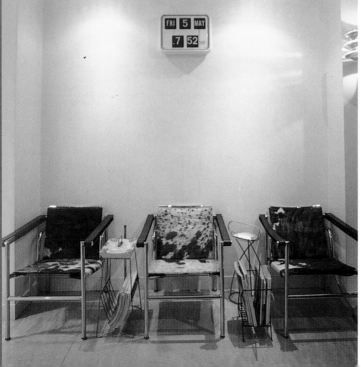

「顧客と店の人間がお互いの好みを分かりあうことがで
きる環境が、良いサービスにつながっていく」をコンセプ
トに、店づくりがなされている美容室。そのこだわりに基
づき、グラフィックや空間を積極的に活用し、独自の世界
を築いている。

A beauty salon built on the concept that "an environment that
facilitates mutual understanding between customers and staff
regarding their respective tastes leads to good service." The
application of this principle in the interior and graphic design
creates a unique realm.

088

パンフレット　Pamplet

ポストカード　Post Card

パンフレット　Pamplet

ケーツー　K. two　Japan

大阪府大阪市中央区西心斎橋2-4-2 難波日興ビル2F
2F Namba Nikko-Bldg., 2-4-2 Nishi-Shinsaibashi Chuo-ku
Osaka-shi Osaka

A：	文田昭仁　Akihito Fumita
AD, D：	芦谷正人　Masato Ashitani
P：	田中マサアキ　Masaaki Tanaka
CW：	観音寺 竜之輔　Ryunosuke Kannonji
Artist：	伊庭靖子　Yasuko Iba
DF：	ドライブ　Drive

会社案内　Brochure

年賀状　New Year's Card

120坪の大型ヘアサロン。アート、建築、デザインなどから
インスパイアされたヘアスタイル、ライフスタイルを提案。
顧客の待ち合い室をギャラリーとして使用し、ショッピン
グバッグには展示作家の作品を刷り込んでいる。

A spacious, almost 400-sq. meter beauty salon proposing
hair/life styles inspired by art, architecture, and design. The
waiting room doubles as gallery; works on exhibit are printed
on the shopping bags.

パスム　PASM　Japan

東京都港区北青山3-8-3 B1F
B1F, 3-8-3 Kita-Aoyama Minato-ku Tokyo

　　A：城戸崎 和佐　Nagisa Kidosaki
　　AF：城戸崎和佐建築設計事務所　Nagisa Kidosaki Office
CD, AD：水谷孝次　Koji Mizutani
　　I：カヨ・アイバ　Kayo Aiba
　　DF：水谷事務所　Mizutani Studio

ポストカード　Post Card

最新モードのヘアスタイルを気持ちのいい空間の中で提案できる店づくりを目指している。女性に居心地いいと思ってもらえるように、優しさとかわいらしさをイラストレーションに託して、ラブリーな空間を演出している。

The latest in hair styling offered in a pleasant-feeling atmosphere. Sweet and gentle illustrations are used to create a lovely interior that women perceive as nice to be in.

衣
Clothing

ブティック
Boutiques

● 総合衣料　　　　　Clothing
● レディースウエア　Women's Clothing
● メンズウエア　　　Men's Clothing
● 子供服　　　　　　Children's Clothing
● 古着　　　　　　　Used Clothing

ファイナル ホーム　FINAL HOME　Japan
東京都港区南青山5-6-5
5-6-5 Minami-Aoyama Minato-ku Tokyo

CD, AD：黒田益朗　Masuo Kuroda（1）
　　D：津村耕佑　Kosuke Tsumura
　　P：ホンマタカシ　Takashi Homma（1）

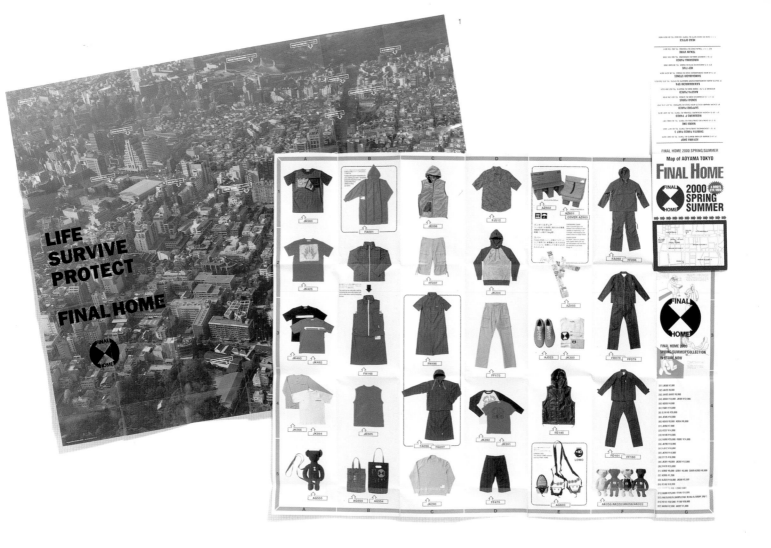

ポストカード　Post Card

ブランドコンセプトの「life, survive, protect」を体現化したオリジナル商品を扱うブティック。ショッピングバッグにリサイクル利用を考えたクラフト紙を使用したり、商品の用途をイラストで紹介するなど、様々なこだわりが見える。

A boutique offering original products that embody the brand concept "live, survive, protect" as evidenced in recyclable kraft paper shopping, illustrations presenting suggested product uses, and a variety of other design details.

ムークス　MOOKS　Japan

東京都渋谷区恵比寿南3-2-16 オクトピア恵比寿南
Octopia Ebisu-minami, 3-2-16 Ebisu-minami
Shibuya-ku Tokyo

A, AD： リチャード・アラン　Richard Allan

タグ　Tag

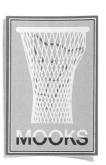

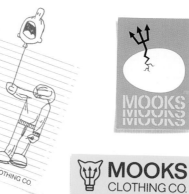

MOOKS CLOTHING CO.

ステッカー　Sticker

MOOKS CLOTHING CO

オーストラリアで誕生したストリートブランドの服を
扱うオンリーショップ。いまの若者たちの気分を表現し
たグラフィックデザインを展開しており、ロゴマークに
使用されているlight bulb（電球）モチーフの新しい解釈
も新鮮である。

The only retail store of a street-brand of clothing originating
in Australia. The new interpretation of the light bulb, as used
in the logomark, is as fresh as the rest of their distinctive
graphic design, expressing the spirit of youth today.

クラッチ　CLUTCH　Japan

東京都渋谷区宇田川町2-1 UP'S 4
UP'S 4, 2-1 Udagawa-cho Shibuya-ku Tokyo

A：野口浩臣　Hiroomi Noguchi
AF：アイ・オール　I-Ole
CD, AD, D：服部富美子　Fumiko Hattori
CD, AD, D：アントニオ・デザイン・サービス　A. D. S. (2)
CD：ソニア・パーク　Sonya S. Park (1)
D：関口修男　Nobuo Sekiguchi (1)
平林奈緒美　Naomi Hirabayashi (1)
P：石田 東　Higashi Ishida (1)

ラベル　Label

ファッションと音楽をリンクさせた新しいライフ
スタイルを、服で表現するブランドの路面店は、音
楽色の強い店内構成になっている。有名スタイリス
トが編集長を務めるカルチャーマガジンをスポン
サードするなど、文化活動にも力を入れている。

The interior of this street-level store, for a fashion brand
proposing a new lifestyle linking fashion and music as
expressed through clothing, is imbued with the flavor of
music. High priority has been given to supporting cultural
activities, including sponsorship of a culture magazine,
the managing editor of which is a celebrated stylist.

ブルーヘブン プールス
Blue Heaven Pools　Japan

東京都世田谷区北沢2-33-12 2F
2F, 2-33-12 Kitazawa Setagaya-ku Tokyo

AD： 橋本公次　Koji Hashimoto
　D： 北華阿飛　Afei Kitahana
　DF： 北華 阿飛 世界　Kitahana Afei Mandalas

ポストカード　Post Card

ショップカード　Shop Card

ラベル　Label

アジアンテイストのイラストを使ったグラフィックデザイン、商品展開をしているメンズブティック。アジアの様々な宗教、美術、文字、文化、文様などを大胆に取り入れ、「聖と俗」「麗と醜」など相反する世界を表現している。

A men's boutique with graphic design and product development based on Asian illustration. Asian religions, art, letterforms, and motifs are boldly used to express antithetical realms such as "sacred and vulgar," "beautiful and ugly."

ジンゴ JINGO Japan

東京都渋谷区神宮前5-30-2 第一タカラビル202
202 Daiichi Takara-Bldg., 5-30-2 Jingumae Shibuya-ku Tokyo

A, AD, D, CW：濱田信英 Nobuhide Hamada

フライヤー Flyer

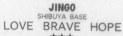

JINGO
SHIBUYA BASE
LOVE BRAVE HOPE
★★★
#202 DAIICHI TAKARA Bld
5-30-2 JINGUMAE SHIBUYAKU TOKYO
150-0001 JAPAN
TEL 03-5468-1822

ポストカード Post Card

店内にある商品は全てオリジナル。西洋文化の産物である
Tシャツに、独自にあみ出したメッセージをのせて日本流
にデザインし、このショップが考える現代感覚の日本文化
を表現している。店名は「強硬論的愛国主義者」を意味する。

T-shirts, an outgrowth of Western culture, designed Japanese
style and printed with uniquely devised messages, each an
original. The shop is a direct expression of the present-day
Japanese cultural sensibilities that conceived it; the store name
means "hard-line nationalist."

ムーン　moon　Japan

東京都渋谷区神宮前2-24-6 第2里見ビル1F
1F Daini Satomi-Bldg., 2-24-6 Jingumae Shibuya-ku Tokyo

D：ドップ　Dop

ステッカー　Sticker

ドイツ語で「自分と同じ容姿をした悪霊」という意味を持つブランドのオンリーショップは、光ではなく陰の世界をイメージしたデザインになっている。ブランドコンセプトは、アンダーグラウンドで狭く深いファンに向けた、オリジナリティのある服づくり。

The only retail shop of a fashion brand, which in German means "evil spirit that looks like me," is designed to express the world of shadow. Based on the concept "underground," their original approach is targeted to a narrow but hardcore following.

雑誌広告　Magazine Ad

ハンジロー セントラル
HANJIRO CENTRAL　Japan
東京都渋谷区神宮前1-6-1 パレフランス4F
4F Palais France, 1-6-1 Jingumae Shibuya-ku Tokyo

　A： 渡辺 浩　Hiroshi Watanabe
AF： 三本菅デザイン事務所　Sanbonsuge Design Office

ポストカード　Post Card

会員証
Member's Card

ショップカード
Shop Card

スーパーマーケットのように広い店内で、世界各国から
集められた古着、ファッション小物、雑貨などを販売。
「自由な発想により本来のデザインや使用目的を変える」
をコンセプトとして、古着店の新しい形を提案している。

Used clothing, accessories, and housewares using materials
from around the world sold in a space the size of a
supermarket. A new-type variety store based on the concept
of "free-thinking changing the initial design and intended use."

パーグラムマーケット
Per Gramme Market Japan
東京都目黒区上目黒1-6-5 森ビル1F
1F Mori-Bldg., 1-6-5 Kamimeguro Meguro-ku Tokyo

A： 清水竜也 Tatsuya Shimizu
AF： リザード Lizard
AD, D： 永森敬子 Keiko Nagamori

ヨーロッパで古着を買い付けて1g＝¥8という一定価格
で商品を販売する、日本で初めての量り売りのブティッ
ク。量りをモチーフにしたロゴマークが、このショップ
のコンセプトを明確に表現している。

Secondhand clothes bought in Europe sold at 8 yen/gram in
Japan's first boutique to sell clothing by weight. The scale motif
used in the logomark distinctly expresses the store concept.

ポストカード Post Card

フライヤー Flyer

マッド　Mudd　Japan

東京都目黒区自由が丘2-8-15
2-8-15 Jiyugaoka Meguro-ku Tokyo

AF：	㈱ゼスト　Zest Co., Ltd.
CD, AD：	水谷孝次　Koji Mizutani
D：	遠藤一成　Kazunari Endo
P：	越谷喜隆　Yoshitaka Koshiya
Hair-make：	沢田哲哉　Tetsuya Sawada
DF：	水谷事務所　Mizutani Studio

ポストカード　Post Card

カタログ　Catalog

ニューヨークで人気を集めているインディーズブランド
の日本初上陸店。「トレンドに左右されてはいけない。ス
タイルは自分で決めなさい」というメッセージが、ティー
ンズゼネレーションのハートをつかみ急成長。アーティ
ストたちからも支持を集めている。

The popular New York independent brand makes its first
appearance in Japan. Messages like "don't be influenced by
trend" and "create your own style" grabbed the teen-generation's
heart and took off. The brand draws support from artists as well.

ランドリー Laundry Japan

東京都渋谷区神南1-9-7 丸栄ビル203
203 Maruei-Bldg., 1-9-7 Jinnan Shibuya-ku Tokyo

AF : ㈱マチス・デザイン・オフィス
　　 Matis Design Office Co., Ltd.

ポストカード　Post Card

ラベル　Label

「洗濯物、洗濯場」という意味の店名を持つ、Tシャツの
セレクトショップ。イラストからグラフィックデザイン
ものまで、幅広いジャンルのプリントTシャツを取り扱
うショップらしく、ラフで気取らない内装が温かみのあ
る空間をつくり出している。

Befitting of a shop offering multi-genre "select" T-shirts
hosting illustrations and other printed graphics, the rough-
hewn, unassuming interior decor creates a warm space.

ピュアルセシン　pual ce cin　Japan
東京都中央区銀座3-2-1 ブランタン銀座
Printemps Ginza, 3-2-1 Ginza Chuo-ku Tokyo

A：河崎和浩　Kazuhiro Kawasaki
AF：河崎デザインスタジオ　Kawasaki Design Studio

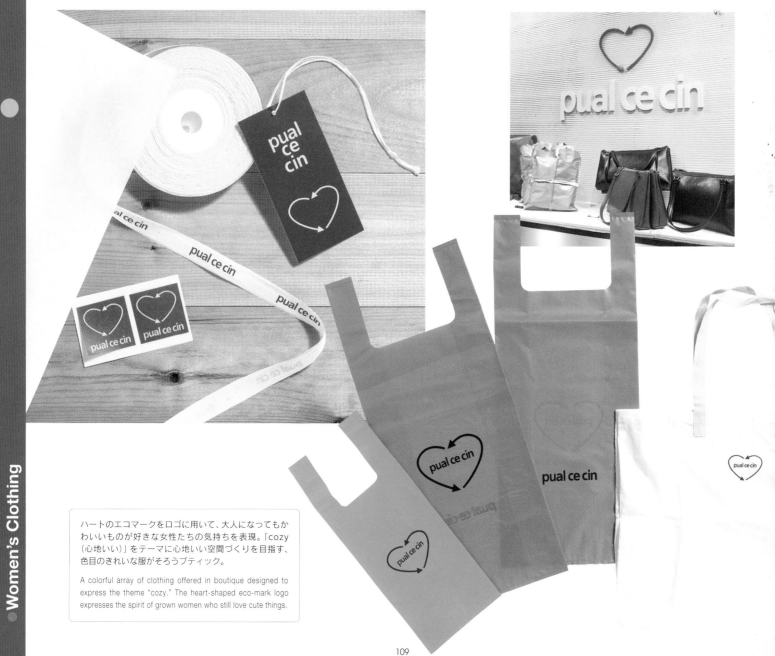

ハートのエコマークをロゴに用いて、大人になってもかわいいものが好きな女性たちの気持ちを表現。「cozy（心地いい）」をテーマに心地いい空間づくりを目指す、色目のきれいな服がそろうブティック。

A colorful array of clothing offered in boutique designed to express the theme "cozy." The heart-shaped eco-mark logo expresses the spirit of grown women who still love cute things.

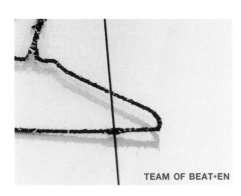

ティーム・オブ・ビートン TEAM OF BEATEN Japan

東京都渋谷区宇田川町14-5 渋谷パルコ Part 3 2F
2F Shibuya Parco Part-3, 14-5 Udagawa-cho Shibuya-ku Tokyo

AF：㈱マチス・デザイン・オフィス Matis Design Office Co., Ltd.

ラベル Label

ボーイッシュで動きやすいウエアを中心に展開しながら、小物にアクセントを置いた遊び心のあるコーディネイトを女性に提案。ブランドコンセプトと同様、グラフィックツールにも遊び心が満載。

A look that coordinates boyish, non-restricting clothes with accessories that create a playful accent. The graphic tools are replete with the same playfulness as the brand concept.

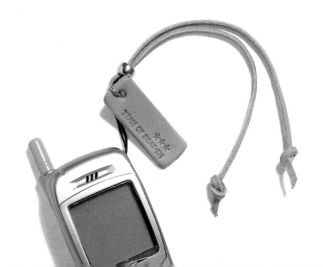

クラスシックス　clas:six　Japan

東京都渋谷区猿楽町4-5 J&HビルB1F
B1F J&H-Bldg., 4-5 Sarugaku-cho Shibuya-ku Tokyo

A : 山下隆生　Takao Yamashita
AF : ㈱英進　Space Creation Eishin
CD, AD, D : 山下隆生　Takao Yamashita
DF : ㈲ビューティ ビースト
Beauty:Beast Ltd.

タグ　Tag

「揺りかごから墓場まで」をコンセプトに、アパレルブランド『beauty:beast』のミュージアムショップとしてオープン。年代やシーズンを超越したこれまでの10年間の作品と、この店オリジナルの商品を販売している。

A museum-like shop opened by apparel brand "Beauty: Beast" based on the concept "from the cradle to the grave" offers clothing that transcended age and season for the past ten years, as well as new original items.

ドゥヴィネット オーグ　DEVINETTE+　Japan
東京都渋谷区猿楽町28-2 SPEAK FOR 1F
1F Speak For, 28-2 Sarugaku-cho Shibuya-ku Tokyo

A：倉島栄二　Eiji Kurashima
AF：倉島栄二デザイン事務所　Eiji Kurashima Design Office
AD, P：モート・シュナーベル　Mote Schnabel (1)
DF：スーパーチャージャー　Supercharger (1)

1　写真集　Photography Book

ポストカード　Post Card

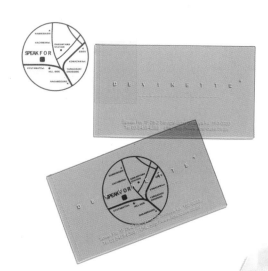

時代性をキャッチしたオリジナル商品のほか、海外若手アーティストが手掛けた服、雑貨、アクセサリーなど、『ドゥヴィネット』の世界観とリンクするアイテムをセレクトしたブティック。服とアートの融合を提案している。

Original products that capture the spirit of the times, clothing by young international artists, sundries, and accessories; a boutique that offers a selection of items representing Devinette+'s view of the world — the fusion of fashion and art.

パンフレット　Pamphlet

シンイチロウ アラカワ
SHINICHIRO ARAKAWA　Japan
東京都渋谷区神宮前3-29-3
3-29-3 Jingumae Shibuya-ku Tokyo

D：荒川眞一郎　Shinichiro Arakawa

招待状　Invitation Card

タグ Tag

フランスの伝統色にあるような、ちょっと青みがかった白で店内を統一し、オープンなイメージに仕上げたブティック。レディースはボルドー、メンズはグリーンというようにタグを色分けするなど、様々なシーンで色をポイントとして使用している。

The boutique interior is finished in bluish white (a traditional French color) which unifies the space and creates a sense of openness. Color is used as a variety of accents, such as in differentiating men's and women's clothing with green and burgundy tags respectively.

ゼロ　ZERO　USA

225 Mott Street, New York, NY 10012

CD, AD, D：マーク・ホフマン　Marc Hohmann (1,2,3)
CD, AD, P, CW：マーク・ボースウィック　Mark Borthwick (1)
CD, AD, D：アキコ・ツジ　Akiko Tsuji (2,3)
D：アキコ・ツジ　Akiko Tsuji (1)
P：マーク・ホフマン　Marc Hohmann (2)
DF：コン/ストラクター　Kon/Struktur

ファッション、デザイン、写真のニューウェイブを、「洗練と即興性の融合」をテーマに提示。ロゴマークは、Tシャツ、バッグ、案内状に必ず使われるドレイプのついた生地、カット、形態を表している。店舗やデザイナーの名前以上に目だつロゴは店舗の空間や名前に対する「ノーイメージ」という戦略に添った認識を高めている。

Zero presents a "new wave" of cutting-edge fashion, design, and photography in which refinement meets improvisation. The logomark expresses draped fabrics, cuts and forms; a consistent element casually applied to T-shirts, bags, and invitations. Its prominent use over the store and designers' names enhances recognition in parallel to the "no image" approach to the store space and name.

1　カタログ　Catalog

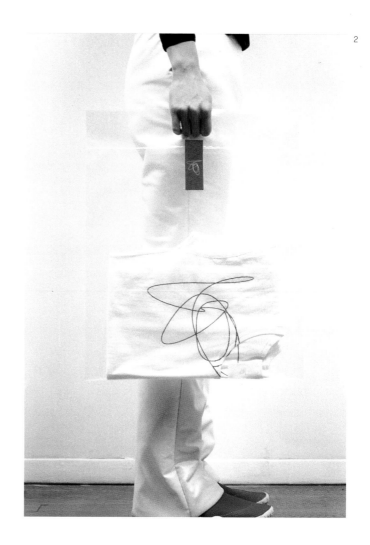

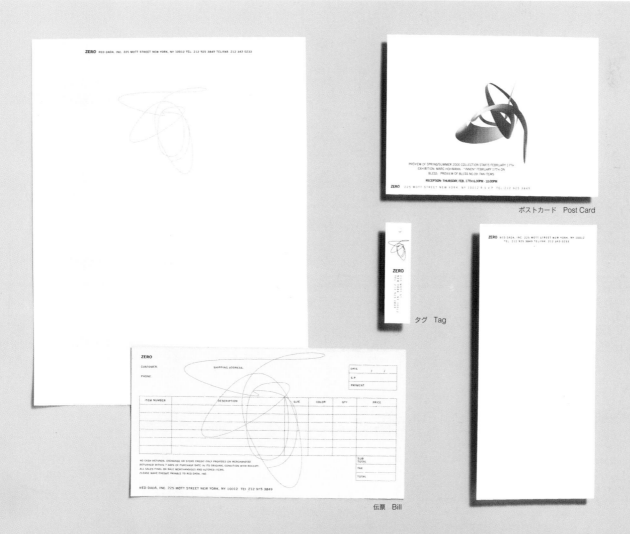

ポストカード　Post Card

タグ　Tag

伝票　Bill

ブルー BLUE Austria
Am Marktplatz, Dornbirn 6850

CD, AD, D, CW： ステファン・サグマイスター Stefan Sagmeister
D： エリック・ジム Eric Zim
P： トム・シャーリッツ Tom Schierlitz
I： カミール・ヴァイナー Kamil Vajnar
DF： サグマイスター Sagmeister Inc.

ファッションチェーン、『ブルー』ではグラフィックツール及びパッケージにはじまり、ストアインテリアまで全てのイメージがオレンジ色でデザインされている。このコンセプトは店の個性に強いインパクトを与えている。

All image-related applications from identity and packaging to store interior for fashion chain called "Blue" are designed in orange. The concept gives the shop identity a strong impact.

アルバローザ マイ・タネ
Alba Rosa My Tane Japan
東京都渋谷区神宮前6-29-10
6-29-10 Jingumae Shibuya-ku Tokyo

A : 柿谷耕司 Koji Kakitani
　　本木朱実 Akemi Motoki
AF : ㈲柿谷耕司アトリエ Koji Kakitani Atelier
AD : 橋本季楊子 Kiyoko Hashimoto
LD : 辻 悠次 Yuji Tsuji
DF : ロケット Rockett

ポストカード　Post Card

ステッカー　Sticker

ショップカード　Shop Card

サーファーが持つ解放感、共生感、遊び心、冒険心と、彼らのライフスタイルをイメージした商品展開をしているメンズブティック。「エモーショナルトリップ」というコンセプトのもと、ポリネシア語で「私の彼」という意味を持つブランド名がつけられた。

A men's boutique offering an array of products that express the freedom, symbiosis, playfulness, and adventure surfers embody and the image of their lifestyle. The brand name, which means "my man" in Polynesian, supports the "emotional trip" concept.

シャンハイ・タン **SHANGHAI TANG** China
Pedder Bldg., 12 Pedder Street, Central, Hong Kong

ポストカード　Post Card

ポストカード　Post Card

ステッカー　Sticker

伝統的中国文化と20世紀の活力を織り交ぜ、中国のデザインに新しい力を与えているショップ。主力店は香港中心部の歴史的建造物の1400m²を占めており、二層の全フロアには伝統的中国の装飾と現代中国美術が並置され、活き活きとした魅力をあふれさせている。

Shanghai Tang revitalizes Chinese design by interweaving traditional Chinese culture with twentieth-century dynamism. The flagship store occupies 15,000 sq. feet of a historic building in Central Hong Kong. Two full floors exude vibrant charm, juxtaposing traditional Chinese decor with contemporary Chinese art.

ミクスト　Mixte　Japan

東京都渋谷区宇田川町15-1 渋谷パルコ Part1 4F
4F Shibuya Parco Part-1, 15-1 Udagawa-cho Shibuya-ku Tokyo

AF：㈱マチス・デザイン・オフィス　Matis Design Office Co., Ltd.

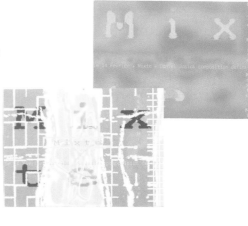

ポストカード　Post Card

「トレンドに振り回されない」をキーワードにした衣料の
セレクトショップ。シンプルなグラフィックデザインが
ブランドコンセプトを表現している。

A shop offering "select" clothing "not tossed about by trend."
Simple graphics express the brand concept.

ショップカード　Shop Card

Mixte DANS l'ÉTÉ 1998.
CUBANGRAPH.

PHOTOGRAPHE HIBIKI KOBAYASHI

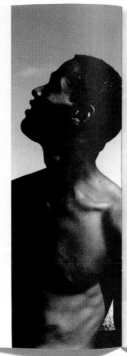

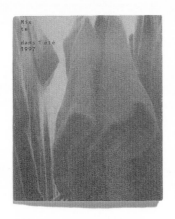

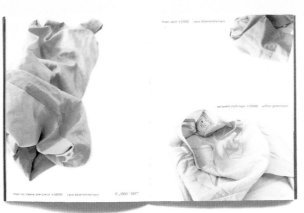

カタログ Catalog

イー　E　Japan

東京都中央区銀座7-8-13 中泉ビル1F
1F Nakaizumi-Bldg., 7-8-13 Ginza Chuo-ku Tokyo

A：竹野 誠　Makoto Takeno
AF：竹野デザインワークス　Takeno Design Works
P：ロレンツォ・マルクッチ　Lorenzo Marcucci (1)
DF：スペースE　Space E

招待状　Invitation Card

1　カタログ　Catalog

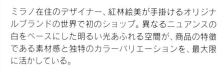

ミラノ在住のデザイナー、紅林絵美が手掛けるオリジナルブランドの世界で初のショップ。異なるニュアンスの白をベースにした明るい光あふれる空間が、商品の特徴である素材感と独特のカラーバリエーションを、最大限に活かしている。

The first retail store for an original brand by Milan-based designer Emi Kurebayashi. The light-filled, basically white space shows off the distinctive materials and color variations characteristic of the products to their fullest.

ノーリーズ　NOLLEY'S　Japan

東京都渋谷区神南1-19-3
1-19-3 Jinnan Shibuya-ku Tokyo

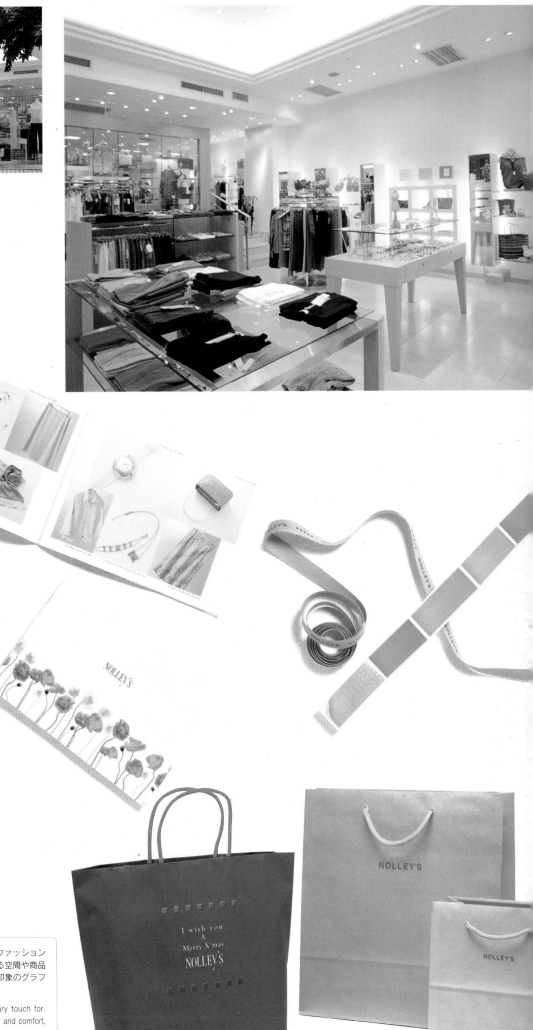

クリスマスカード
Christmas Card

シンプルなスタイルに時代性をプラスしたファッション
を発信。「心地良さ」「質の良さ」が感じられる空間や商品
を提案しているショップらしく、さわやかな印象のグラフ
ィックデザインが好感度高い。

Stylistically simple fashion with a contemporary touch for.
Befitting a store and products that exude quality and comfort,
the fresh-feeling graphic design makes a favorable impression.

ポストカード　Post Card

ショップカード　Shop Card

インデックス　INDEX　Japan

東京都渋谷区神宮前6-5-6
6-5-6 Jingumae Shibuya-ku Tokyo

D：ファビアン・モンハイン　Fabien Monhein
　　ソフィア・ウッド　Sophia Wood
DF：フライ　Fly

エアポートをイメージして設計された店内に並ぶのは、
流行を意識した服とファッションアクセサリー。この店
は道路に面した部分が全面ガラス張りになっており、白
を基調としたクリーンな店内には、あふれんばかりの自
然光が注ぎこんでいる。

Trend-conscious clothing and accessories line a store interior
imaged after an airport. Natural light floods the clean,
fundamentally white interior through an all-glass storefront.

ダブル アール　WR　Japan
東京都渋谷区代官山町13-4 ヴォーグ代官山Ⅱ1F
1F Vogue Daikanyama-Ⅱ, Daikanyama-cho
Shibuya-ku Tokyo

ポストカード　Post Card

「ある1人の女性の日常」をテーマにファッションアイテムを提供するブティックは、彼女の部屋を再現することをコンセプトに、可動式の什器を使用し、店内はいつでもレイアウト変更可能。ショップカラーの茶と青は、大地と空をイメージしている。

A boutique offering fashion items based on the theme "a day in the life of a woman"; the store interior recreates "her" room. Movable fixtures make layout changes possible at any time. The shop colors, brown and blue, represent the earth and sky.

グレース　GRACE　Japan

東京都渋谷区鴬谷町12-5 大芦ビル1F
1F Oashi-Bldg., 12-5 Uguisudani-cho Shibuya-ku Tokyo

AD： 岡本克喜　Katsuyoshi Okamoto (1)
　D： 堀井敏也　Toshiya Horii (1)
　P： 石田晃久　Akihisa Ishida (1)
DF： ㈱カーツ　Karhtu (1)

1　ポストカード

クラシカルな雰囲気の店内と、世界の伝統的な技術を織り込んだオリジナル商品が個性的なブティック。世界各地から新鮮な素材を探し出して商品を製作し、独特のクラシック・ファッシンスタイルを展開している。

A distinctive boutique with a classical atmosphere offering original items that incorporate traditional techniques and materials from around the world to create a unique style of classic fashion.

ウサギ・プゥ・エル　Usagi POUR ELLE　Japan

東京都渋谷区神宮前1-11-6 ラフォーレ原宿3.5F
3.5F Laforet Harajuku, 1-11-6 Jingumae Shibuya-ku Tokyo

D： ナタリー・レテ　Nathalié Leté

ポストカード　Post Card

ステッカー　Sticker

「パリの日常の中にあるクリエイティブ」を感じさせる
ファッションアイテム,小物などをセレクトして販売する、
若い女性をターゲットにしたブティック。店名になってい
る「うさぎ」のイラストをグラフィックに使用し、ショッ
プの持つガーリッシュなイメージを強調している。

A boutique offering select fashion items and knickknacks that
embody the "quality of Parisian living," targeted to young
women. The girlish image livens up the store interior, as does
the rabbit logo expressing the store name.

アリィツィア　aritzia　Canada

CD, D： トロイ・ベイリー　Troy Bailly
AD： デビッド・パピニュー　David Papineau
　　　ステファン・パークス　Stephen Parkes
DF： プロトタイプ・デザイン　Prototype Design

ポストカード　Post Card

モダンなラインと自然素材の衣料は、欧米社会では珍しく女性を買い物に熱狂させる。

The modern lines and natural textures drive women into a wild shopping frenzy unparalleled in the Western world.

クチャ　cuccia　Japan
東京都渋谷区宇田川町15-1 渋谷パルコ Part 1 1F
1F Shibuya Parco Part-1, 15-1 Udagawa-cho Shibuya-ku Tokyo

AF：㈱マチス・デザイン・オフィス　Matis Design Office Co., Ltd.

無国籍で女性的な雰囲気を漂わせる店内で扱っているアイテムは、ブランドテーマの「散歩」から発想される様々なシチュエーションに合った服とファッション小物。グラフィックデザインにもガーリッシュ感覚があふれている。

Clothing and accessories related to a variety of imaginable situations based on the brand theme "a walk," offered in an ethnic and feminine store atmosphere. The graphic design also brims over with girlishness.

カタログ　Catalog

ステッカー　Sticker

ポストカード　Post Card

1998 cuccia spring & summer

ロペ ピクニック　Ropé Picnic　Japan

東京都江東区青海1丁目パレットタウン1370
1370 Palette Town, 1 Aomi Koto-ku Tokyo

Interior Designer : 津村将勝　Masakatsu Tsumura
CD, AD, D : 渡辺陽子　Yoko Watanabe
D : 田中陽子　Yoko Tanaka
P : 中村和孝　Kazutaka Nakamura
LD, I : フランソワ・アヴリル　François Avril
DF : ㈱ジュン ロペ事業部
Jun Co., Ltd. Ropé Division

フレンチテイストのコーディネートを提案するブティック。フランス人アーティストが手掛けたロゴは、おしゃれをして犬を散歩させる女性の姿。ブランド名の「ピクニック」という言葉が持つ、ワクワクするような気分を表現したグラフィックデザインが楽しい。

The image of a well-dressed lady walking a dog created by a French artist forms the logo for a boutique offering French-style coordinate fashions. The fun-filled graphic design expresses the same spirit of excitement that the store name "picnic" inspires.

カタログ　Catalog

ポストカード
Post Card

メープル クリークス
MAPLE CREEKS Japan
東京都渋谷区神宮前1-11-6 ラフォーレ原宿1.5F
1.5F Laforet Harajuku, 1-11-6 Jingumae Shibuya-ku Tokyo

A：金本有加 Yuka Kanemoto
AF：マウンテンファイブ Mountain Five

ラベル Label

原宿の流行発信源『ラフォーレ原宿』の中にあるこの
ショップでは、シンプルな女性の美しさをイメージした
グラフィックを展開。時代のトレンドやエッセンスをさ
りげなく取り入れた、気取りのないおしゃれが楽しめる
日常着を提案している。

A shop in trendsetting LaForet Harajuku that offers an
unassuming dressiness in everyday wear while subtly
adopting the trends and essence of the times. Simple
graphics express a woman's underlying beauty.

カタログ Catalog

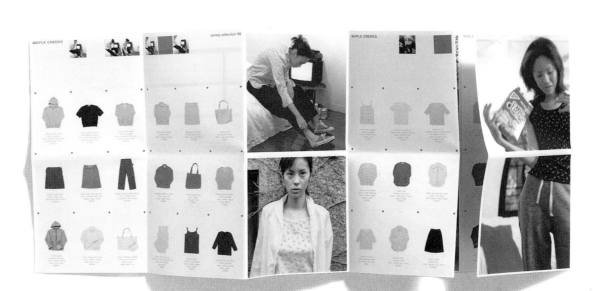

ハナ　HANA　Japan

東京都渋谷区神南1-9-7 丸栄ビル104
104 Maruei-Bldg., 1-9-7 Jinnan Shibuya-ku Tokyo

AF：㈱マチス・デザイン・オフィス
　　　Matis Design Office Co., Ltd.

ステッカー　Sticker

ラベル　Label

ショップカード　Shop Card

「heart, antique, native, all world」をキーワードに、花
をイメージするファッション・アイテムとアンティークの
小物を展開。そのコンセプトはウッディな店内、店名、花
のイラストを使用したグラフィックツールにも反映され
ている。

Floral-motif fashion items and antique knickknacks
expressing the key words "heart, antique, native and all-
world." The concept is reflected in the woody store interior,
store name, and graphic tools featuring floral illustrations.

ジーン・ナッソーズ リテイルストア
JEAN NASSAUS RETAIL STORE　Japan
東京都渋谷区恵比寿西1-34-23 代官山トキビル2F
2F Daikanyama Toki-Bldg., 1-34-23 Ebisu-nishi Shibuya-ku Tokyo

A： 小石川直記　Naoki Koishikawa
AF： ㈱ワクト　Wact
D： 室井 幸　Miyuki Muroi

ステッカー　Sticker

カリフォルニアのウエストコーストやハワイのラハイナ
を感じさせる、パシフィックスタイルにこだわったブ
ティック。「アウトドア、ハワイアン、70'S」のブランド
イメージを、グラフィックツールにバンダナの花柄を使
用することで表現している。

A Pacific-style boutique that has the feeling of Lahaina,
Hawaii or the California West Coast. The graphics incorporate
floral patterns often seen on Hawaiian scarves to express the
brand image, "outdoor, Hawaiian, 70s."

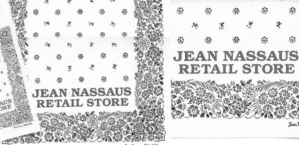

ル プティ ブルー　Le petit Bleu　Japan
東京都渋谷区恵比寿西1-21-5 大野ビル1F
1F Ono-Bldg., 1-21-5 Ebisu-nishi Shibuya-ku Tokyo

　A：土田久雄　Hisao Tsuchida
AF：㈱ヰノセント　Innocent Inc.

ステッカー　Sticker

ラベル　Label

「大人のかわいらしさを持ちつつ、他にない個性を感じさせる服」をテーマに、フランスからのインポートや国内のデザイナーズブランドものを中心にセレクト。ショップの外観、グラフィックツールのイメージどおり、きれいな色目のアイテムが充実している。

A selection of imported French and Japanese designer brands that fit the theme "clothing with an adult sense of sweetness and individuality unlike any other." As reflected the shop exterior and graphic tools, the shop offers a substantial array of items in beautiful colors.

ニーム NÎMES Japan

東京都渋谷区猿楽町26-11 ノブハウス
Nob House, 26-11 Sarugaku-cho Shibuya-ku Tokyo

A： 土田久雄 Hisao Tsuchida
AF： ㈱ヰノセント Innocent Inc.

ステッカー Sticker

フレンチテイストをキーワードに、カジュアルなファッション
アイテムを展開。素材にこだわり、着心地がよく、着回しのき
く服がそろう。そのイメージに合わせ、グラフィックツールも
ホッとするような優しい雰囲気に仕上げている。

"French taste" is the basis of a line of casual items; a collection of
clothing that shows particularity about materials, is versatile and
comfortable to wear. The graphic tools accent the relaxed and
gentle feeling.

ブチバトー ブティック
PETIT BATEAU BOUTIQUE Japan
東京都世田谷区北沢2-25-7 T&Tビル1F
1F T&T-Bldg., 2-25-7 Kitazawa Setagaya-ku Tokyo

AF：サンドゥグレ Cent Degrés
DF：サンドゥグレ イマージュ Cent Degrés Image

ステッカー　Sticker

ステッカー　Sticker

ステッカー　Sticker

ショップカード
Shop Card

着心地のいい生地を使ったTシャツが人気のフランスで
生まれた子供服のブティック。マリンをテーマに、波、
ボート、魚、ヒトデなど、主役である子供たちの感性を刺
激するデザインモチーフを、店内やグラフィックツール
に散りばめている。

A children's boutique originating in France, popular for its T-
shirts made of comfortable fabrics. The store interior and
graphics are studded with marine-based imagery such as
waves, boats, fish and starfishes, to stimulate the senses of
their principal customers — children.

ム・チャ・チャ ヴェス **muchacha-VES** Japan

大阪府大阪市西区南堀江1-14-1
1-14-1 Minami-Horie Nishi-ku Osaka-shi Osaka

A：新屋昌子 Masako Shinya

ステッカー　Sticker

ラベル　Label

気軽に遊びに行ける友だちの家をイメージしてつくられた子供服の店は、あえて看板を出さず、店内にキッチンやトイレのスペースを設けて、親しみのある空間に仕上げている。スマイルマークや花をグラフィックに取り入れたデザインも個性的。

A children's clothing store designed to have the light-hearted feeling of being at a friend's house to play. Including a kitchen and powder room and dispensing with an exterior sign helps give the space a sense of intimacy. Graphics incorporating smile marks and flowers are also distinctive.

9

10

ブー ホームズ　BOO HOMES　Japan
東京都目黒区自由が丘1-24-15 ヒルズ自由が丘C棟
Hills Jiyugaoka-C, 1-24-15
Jiyugaoka Meguro-ku Tokyo

D：宮川 恵　Megumi Miyakawa (1,4)
D, I：鯉渕道生　Michio Koibuchi (2)
D：桜井奈雅子　Nagako Sakurai (3)
D, I：桜井奈雅子　Nagako Sakurai (5)
I：岩橋七世　Nanayo Iwahashi (1,3,4)
DF：㈱ブーフーウー　Boo Foo Woo Co., Ltd.

1　ポストカード　Post Card

ステッカー Sticker

従来の子供服の概念にとらわれず、大人でも欲しくなる
ような本物志向の服、インディアンジュエリーなどを展開
する子供服メーカーのセレクトショップ。ロゴにもなっ
ている豚をモチーフに、色鮮やかなアイテムがあふれる
店内は、親子でワイワイと楽しめる。

A special selection of children's clothes and Indian jewelry
with a "genuine" quality that appeals even to adults. The pig
motif, used in the logo as well, and colorful array of items
make the store interior pleasant for both parent and child.

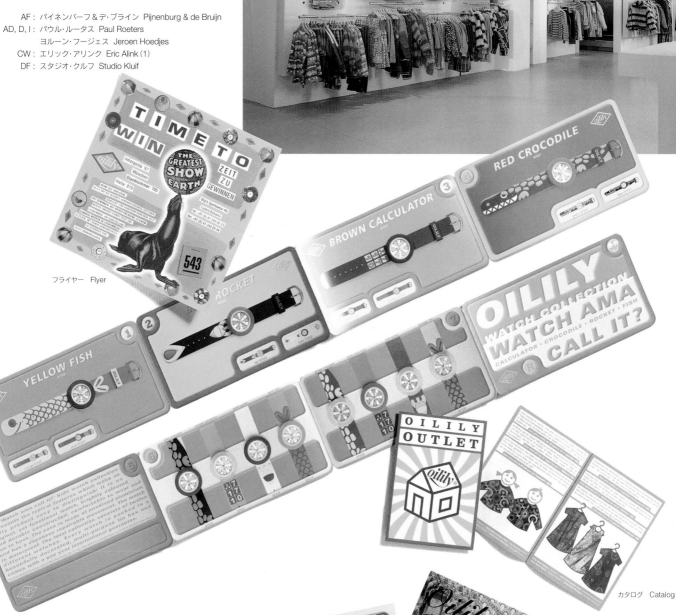

オイリリー　OILILY　The Netherlands

AF：パイネンバーフ＆デ・ブライン　Pijnenburg & de Bruijn
AD, D, I：パウル・ルータス　Paul Roeters
　　　　ヨルーン・フージェス　Jeroen Hoedjes
CW：エリック・アリンク　Eric Alink (1)
DF：スタジオ・クルフ　Studio Kluif

フライヤー　Flyer

カタログ　Catalog

ポストカード　Post Card

『オイリリー』は遊びや子供らしさの要素と、より成熟した実際的なストアデザインとの巧みな調和を創造しており、その店舗はオリジナルの服と同様、カラフルでパワフル。グラフィックスは子供の視点から考え出され、このブランドのファンクラブには総数10万人のメンバーがいる。

Oilily stores are as colorful and powerful as their clothing. Oilily strives to create a fine balance between the playful, childlike elements and more mature, down-to-earth elements of their store design. The graphics are conceived from a child's point of view. Oilily has a fan club 100,000-members strong.

150

ファミリア　familiar　Japan
東京都中央区銀座5-7-10 ニューメルサB1F
B1F New Melsa, 5-7-10 Ginza Chuo-ku Tokyo

A：植木莞爾　Kanji Ueki
CD：八木 保　Tamotsu Yagi

ステッカー　Sticker

子供＆ベビー服を扱う店内は白をベースとし、ピンクや
黄色などのカラーアクセントを効かせて、楽しく元気な
空間に。オリジナルデザインのミネラルウォーターを販
売するウォータバーや、授乳室を設置するなど、親子に
とっての快適な空間を提供している。

Pink, yellow and other colors accent a basically white interior
to create a fun and cheery baby and children's clothes store.
Features such as a bar selling original-label mineral water
and a nursing room enhance the comfort of the store for
parents and children.

152

食
Food
飲食店と食品専門店
Dining and Specialty Food Shops

- カフェ　　　　　　　　Café
- デリ　　　　　　　　　Deli
- レストラン　　　　　　Restaurant
- バー　　　　　　　　　Bar
- ベーカリー　　　　　　Bakery
- ハンバーガー　　　　　Hamburgers
- 練り粉菓子　　　　　　Pastry
- ベーグル　　　　　　　Bagels
- プレッツェル　　　　　Pretzels
- 洋菓子　　　　　　　　Confectionery
- チョコレート　　　　　Chocolates
- 酒　　　　　　　　　　Liquor
- ジュース＆スムージー　Juices & Smoothies
  etc.

フラッグス カフェ　FLAGS Cafe　Japan
東京都新宿区新宿3-28-13 4℃ WOMA新宿店 B1F
B1F 4℃ Woma Shinjuku, 3-28-13 Shinjuku Shinjuku-ku Tokyo

A：高取邦和　Kunikazu Takatori
　　井上 桂　Kei Inoue
AF：㈱高取空間計画　Takatori Kukan Keikaku Inc.
AD, D：駒形克己　Katsumi Komagata

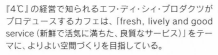

FOOD　お食事

パニーニ　●イタリア風サンドイッチ
ツナ・トマト・チーズのパニーニ　　　　　　¥ 750

カポナータとパルミジャーノのパニーニ
　　　　　　　　　　　　　　　　　　　750

生ハムとモッツアレラのパニーニ
　　　　　　　　　　　　　　　　　　　750

チキン・ベーコン・トマトの
サンドイッチ　　　　　　　　　　　　　850

スモークサーモンとトマトの
タルタルサンドイッチ　　　　　　　　　850

ローストチキンとクルミのサラダ
　　　　　　　　　　　　パン付き　　850

スモークサーモンと
カッテージチーズのサラダ パン付き　850

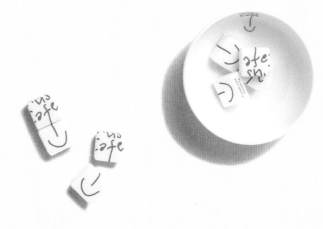

『4℃』の経営で知られるエフ・ディ・シィ・プロダクツが
プロデュースするカフェは、「fresh, lively and good
service（新鮮で活気に満ちた、良質なサービス）」をテー
マに、よりよい空間づくりを目指している。

A café produced by F.D.C. Products Inc. (known for their jewelry
and clothing chain, 4℃) aimed at creating a superior atmosphere
to support the theme "fresh, lively and good service."

コースター Coaster

ショップカード Shop Card

カフェ・ノリータ / デリ・ノリータ
café NOLITA / DELI NOLITA   Japan
東京都渋谷区神宮前1-15-5 Nolita Street Apartment
Nolita Street Apartment, 1-15-5 Jingumae Shibuya-ku Tokyo

同じ建物内のフロア違いにデリとカフェがあり、それぞれのショップに個性的な内装を施している。空間的なくつろぎだけではなく、顧客に満足してもらえる心地いい時間を提供できる店を目指している。

A deli and café, on different floors of the same building, each with distinctive interiors. The spaces are designed to offer customers a comfortable and satisfying experience.

ショップカード　Shop Card

エイ・ディ・ケイ　A.D.K.　Japan
東京都港区南青山5-12-3
5-12-3 Minami-Aoyama Minato-ku Tokyo

AF：㈱ユナイテッド パシフィックス　United Pacifics Co., Ltd.
CD：㈱笄兄弟社　Kougai Brothers & Co.
AD：サイトウ マコト　Makoto Saito
　D：竹田敏彦　Toshihiko Takeda
DF：ホログラム　Hologram

ステッカー　Sticker

メニュー Menu

青山というエリアをひとつの「会社」として考え、その「社員食堂」たりえる土着性の高い飲食店を目指すイタリアンデリ。「顧客が親しみを覚える範囲内で最大限におしゃれ」をテーマに、店舗とグラフィックのデザインがなされている。

An Italian deli that aims to be to the Aoyama area what a "staff dining room" is to a corporation, with a strong sense of indigenousness. The store and graphics are designed to be ultimately chic while providing customers a feeling of intimacy.

ポジティヴ デリ Positive Deli Japan

東京都港区台場1-7 メディアージュ内 3F
3F Mediage, 1-7 Daiba Minato-ku Tokyo

A： 立田一幸 Kazuyuki Tatsuta
AF： 東京家具㈱ Tokyo Kagu Co., Ltd.
CD： 中牟田 洋一（E&Y） Youichi Nakamuta（E&Y）
AD, D, I： アリタ マサフミ Masafumi Arita
DF： ピーディーラブ P/D Lab

東京湾にかかる橋を望める開放的なロケーションのデリ＆カフェということを意識し、優しく清潔感のあるデザインでまとめている。「アボリジナルモダーン」をテーマとしたグラフィックとポップで親しみやすいイラストで全体を構成。

Design for a deli and café located on open-feeling site with a view of a bridge spanning Tokyo Bay is clean and gentle. The overall image is composed of graphics and a likable bop illustration based on the theme "aboriginal modem."

ランチョンマット
Luncheon Mat

コースター Coaster

ラ・サルーテ　La Salute　Japan

東京都新宿区西新宿1-3-14 全研プラザⅢ
Zenken Plaza-Ⅲ, 1-3-14 Nishi-Shinjuku Shinjuku-ku Tokyo

A：清野燿聖　Yosei Kiyono
AF：㈱サンライズ ジャパン　Sunrise Japan Co., Ltd.
CD：坂本應尚　Masahisa Sakamoto
AD：遊垣真男　Masao Yugaki
D：立石佳代　Kayo Tatsuishi／下津夏詞　Natsushi Shimozu
DF：㈱ヘルメス　Hermes Inc.

ショップカード　Shop Card

コースター　Coaster

カジュアルなイタリアンを表現するため、1Fのデリ＆カフェはオレンジ色、2Fのレストランは緑色をグラフィックに使用し、明るい印象に仕上げている。チラシやリーフレットには、あえて薄めの紙を用い、印刷の裏写り具合を味にしている。

Orange used in the first-floor casual Italian deli and café and green graphics used in the second-floor restaurant create a cheerful impression. Leaflets printed on thin paper incorporate the show-through as a graphic element.

ショップカード　Shop Card

コースター　Coaster

メニュー　Menu

アイ・エヌ・カフェ I. N. CAFÉ Japan
東京都世田谷区奥沢15-26-16 自由が丘マスト3F
3F Jiyugaoka Mast, 15-26-15 Okusawa Setagaya-ku Tokyo

メニュー Menu

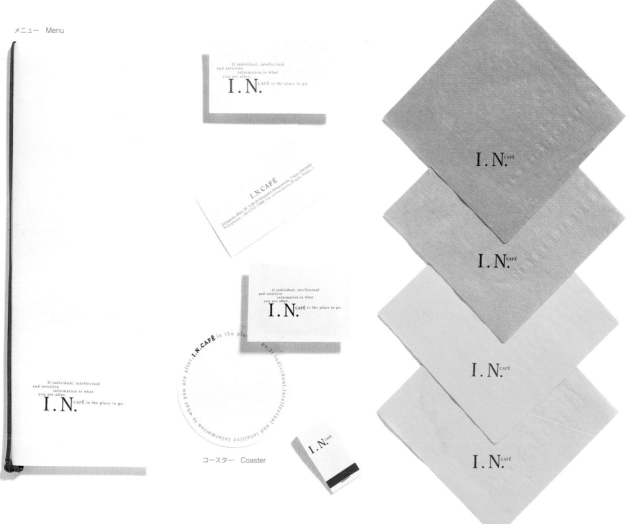

コースター Coaster

ライフスタイル・ショップ『フランフラン』に併設されているライブラリーカフェ。ここの特徴は店内に置かれている洋書を、お茶を飲みながら自由に閲覧できること。グラフィックとともに、白のイメージで統一された店内は開放感がある。

A lively café established by lifestyle shop Franc Franc offering a variety of Western books for perusal while sipping tea. The all-white interior and graphics create a feeling of openness.

ソーザイ　SOZAI　Australia

1221 High Street Armadale, VIC

AF： シックス・ディグリーズ・メルボルン
　　　 Six Degrees Melbourne
CD, AD, D： ジョセフ・コラリック　Joseph Colaric
　　 P： ナオコ・ショウジ　Naoko Shoji
　　　　 ゲン・タバタ　Gen Tabata
　 DF： アトミック・トイ・デザイン　Atomic Toy Design

ポストカード　Post Card

メニュー　Menu

最高級で新鮮な食材を売り物にしている寿司レストラン。料理のみならず視覚的また空間を感じる食事体験を創造するため、素材感、空間、調和感の統合を試みている。

Design for a restaurant committed to using the finest and freshest ingredients combines texture, space, and harmony to create a dining experience based not only on cuisine, but visual and spatial atmosphere as well.

ディッシュ アンド ブックス / カフェ アンド ブックス
dish & books / café & books　Japan

東京都渋谷区神宮前3-25-13 B1F & 3F
B1F & 3F, 3-25-13 Jingumae Shibuya-ku Tokyo

AF：コンテンポラリー プランニング センター
　　　Contemporary Planning Center
A, CD：杉浦 幸　Yuki Sugiura
AD, D：國安 隆　Takashi Kuniyasu
　　P：中道 淳 (ナカサ アンド パートナーズ)
　　　　Jun Nakamichi (Nacása & Partners Inc.)
　　DF：キョウリュウ スタジオ　Kyoryu Studio

ショップカード　Shop Card

ポストカード　Post Card

フレンチを中心としたカジュアルレストランと、気持ち
のいいテラスのあるカフェが、同じ建物内に同居。店内
にディスプレイされている写真集や画集などのビジュア
ル本を見ながら、食事やお茶ができる空間が心地よい。

A casual, French-based restaurant and terrace café sharing
the same architectural space. Art and photography books on
display for perusal while eating or sipping tea create a
pleasant dining atmosphere.

カフェ ボア クレール　café voir clair　Japan

京都府京都市左京区浄土寺西田町112-6
112-6 Nishida-cho Jodoji Sakyo-ku Kyoto-shi Kyoto

ポストカード
Post Card

コースター　Coaster

ステッカー　Sticker

フレンチテイストの眼鏡店『ルネエルネ』がプロデュースするカフェ。目によい素材を食材に入れた料理を企画するなど、普段から視力について考えられる機会を持てるよう、ショップ全体で提案している。

A café produced by the French-taste optical shop Lune et Lune. The shop is designed to raise general awareness about eyesight, including cuisine made with foods considered good for the eyes.

ティー　T　Japan

東京都世田谷区北沢2-34-3 クリスタル・ベスル1F
1F Crystal Vessel, 2-34-3 Kitazawa Setagaya-ku Tokyo

A：金谷隆文　Takafumi Kaneya
AF：タウ設計事務所　Tau Co., Ltd.
D：ダグラス・ドリトル　Douglas Doolittle
DF：DDグラフィックデザインコンサルタント
　　DD Graphic Design Consultant

コースター
Coaster

ランチョンマット　Luncheon Mat

ポストカード　Post Card

オーナーのイニシャルである「T」のみをロゴデザインし
たグラフィックツールが、店内のシンプルなイメージを
反映させている、「くつろぎ」をテーマにしたヨーロピア
ン・スタイルのカフェ＆ダイニングバー。心地よい音楽が
流れる店内は大人のムード満点。

Graphics featuring a logo comprised of just the owner's initial
"T" reflect the simple interior image of a European-style
café/dining bar based on the theme "relaxation."

エル・グロボ　EL GLOBO　Mexico

Av. Popocatepetl, Mexico City 03340

A：アントニオ・ロッツァーノ　Antonio Lozano
CD, D, I：パトリック・バージェフ　Patrick Burgeff
P：マーティン L. バーガス　Martin L. Vargas
DF：バージェフ・グラフィコ　Burgeff Grafiko

メキシコには70を超えるエル・グロボのショップがある。
ロゴは「個性的なクラシックスタイル」というアイディアに
基づいており、ケーキの箱、パンの袋、缶製品のグラフィッ
クスは、100年の伝統、上品な味、高品質を表現している。

There are more than seventy El Globo shops in Mexico. The logo is
based on an idea that looks classic yet has its own personality. The
graphics for cake boxes, bread bags and canned products reflect
over 100 years of tradition, refined taste and excellent quality.

ヒルサイド・パントリー・ウエスト
HILLSIDE PANTRY WEST Japan
東京都渋谷区鉢山13-4 ヒルサイドウエストB棟 B1F
B1F Hillside West-B,
13-4 Hachiyama Shibuya-ku Tokyo

ヨーロッパの街の路地裏にあるようなデリカテッセンを
イメージして、代官山の外れにつくられたこの店は、ク
リーンでホッとできる空間を顧客に提供。息抜きに何度
も訪れたくなる隠れ家のような魅力を振りまいている。

Patterned after a back street European delicatessen, this
clean space on the outskirts of Daikanyama offers customers
a place to relax. Like a hideaway, it has an attractiveness
that makes one want to go back again and again.

フライヤー Flyer

パン工房アンテンドゥ　AntenDo　Japan
東京都武蔵野市吉祥寺南町2-1-3
2-1-3 Kichijoji Minami-machi Musashino-shi Tokyo

これまでに34個の賞に輝く技術の高さと、手間ひまかけ
てつくり上げた個性のあるパンが自慢のベーカリー。
明るく親しみやすい店舗設計、グラフィックデザイン、
元気のいい接客サービスが、入りやすい店の雰囲気づくり
にひと役買っている。

A bakery where technique, time and effort yield the unique baked
goods that have won 34 awards to date. Bright and friendly
interior and graphic design and pleasant customer service, create
a store atmosphere that customers find easy to enter.

171

ベティーズ スイート ファクトリー
Betty's Sweet Factory Japan
愛媛県北条市下難波1427-10
1427-10 Shimonada Hojyo-shi Ehime

A：河野明彦　Akihiko Kono
CD, AD, D, I：八馬 未包子　Mihoko Hachiuma
P：平家康嗣　Yasushi Heike
CW：久保理子　Masako Kubo

カフェレストランのチェーン店が新基軸として展開する
ケーキショップ。欧米の主婦が愛する子供たちにお菓子を
手作りするように、アットホームな空間の中で、甘くしあ
わせなお菓子とくつろぎの時間をこの店は提供している。

A cake shop developed by a café/restaurant chain based on
a new set of criteria. In the kind of at-home atmosphere that
Western mothers enjoy baking with their children, the shop
offers sweet treats and a relaxing time.

PARIS - NEW YORK - TOKYO

リシャール　RICHART　Japan
東京都中央区銀座7-7-12
7-7-12 Ginza Chuo-ku Tokyo

 A： 北澤 聡　Satoru Kitazawa
AF： ㈱アルス ドゥー　Ars Deux Co., Ltd.
 D： ミッシェル・リシャール　Michel Richart
DF： リシャール デザイン エ ショコラ　Richart Design et Chocolat

ステッカー　Sticker

A collection for every occasion

From the simple joy of the slightly sweeter Children's Design Collection to the strong, pure flavors of the Ultra Fines tasting collection, you will find the perfect choice for your most special occasions.

Some selections:

• Saveur d'Automne - a celebration of the tastes of fall, available November-December. Four new flavors are created each year, all based on a seasonally appropriate ingredient, such as the walnut and the chestnut.

RICHART's theme collections.

• O Les Beaux Jours! The fresh flavors of spring, available April through August each year. Again one key spring ingredient is worked into four

32

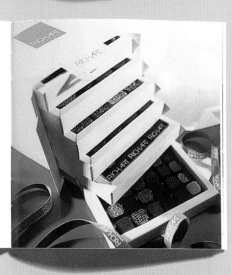

The chocolates are then placed in white, jewel-like Ballotins and sold in RICHART boutiques worldwide in France, Spain, Sweden, Japan and the United States. It's easy to mistake a RICHART boutique for an art gallery. They are minimally designed, clean and stark like the Ballotins, so that the eye is drawn automatically to the main attraction - the chocolate.

To underline the RICHART family's passion for art, the RICHART Design et Chocolat boutiques exhibit the work of local artists. In addition, RICHART organizes an annual Children's Design Contest that benefits elementary school art programs.

The ritual of chocolate.

38

If, indeed, there is a secret at RICHART, it is this : The RICHART family believes that chocolate has a far nobler destination than simply the lips of the chocolate lover. Chocolate should overwhelm his very heart and soul, much as it has overwhelmed the heart and soul of the chocolatier. They believe that chocolate truly can create intense happiness.

And that's why the RICHART collections are so rich in personality. This is why the RICHART family is driven to seek out the highest quality, the most intense originality, a very pure esthetic and the most exquisite presentation. They do it all so that the RICHART collections are as full of character and emotion as chocolate possibly can be.

But the RICHART collections could not be exceptional if you, the people who love and appreciate them, were not extraordinary as well. You, the lovers and connoisseurs of RICHART chocolate, have made it all possible because you so whole-heartedly embraced the RICHART family's vision for a new approach to chocolate.

RICHART chocolate : The Ultimate Pleasure

Thank you.

46

クリエイティブかつオリジナリティあふれる「チョコレートのモダンアート」を目指す、フランス生まれのチョコレート専門店。創業者のミッシェル・リシャールが創造するシンプルで洗練されたデザインが、彼の持つ美的メッセージを表現している。

A French-born chocolate shop producing original and creative "chocolate modern art." Founder Michel Richart's simple and refined design expresses his aesthetic message.

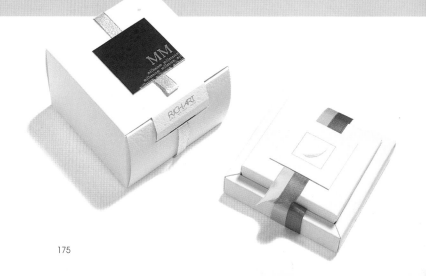

DES PRÉS CAFÉ

TAKE OUT MENU

デ・プレ・カフェ＋パンヤ・デ・プレ
DES PRÉS CAFÉ + PANYA DES PRÉS　Japan
東京都目黒区自由が丘2-16-10 メープルファーム内
Maple Firm, 2-16-10 Jiyugaoka Meguro-ku Tokyo

AD, D：西村 武　Takeshi Nishimura
DF：㈲コンプレイト　Completo Inc.

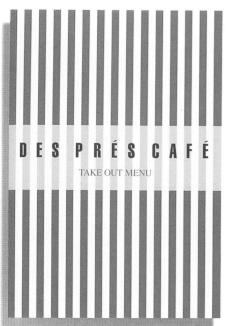

DES PRÉS CAFÉ
TAKE OUT MENU

DES PRÉS CAFÉ

3F DES PRÉS CAFÉにてサンドウィッチ、サラダのTAKE OUTを承っております。ぜひご利用下さい。TEL.FAXでもご注文をお受けいたします。お届けはできませんのでご了承ください。

MENU

【BREAD & SANDWICH】

1. BREAD [ブレッド] ¥300
   (自家製パン・トラ・トレ・パン・リング・ヴィエノワ他)
2. SAINTS. PÉRES SANDWICH [MEAT] [サンペール サンドウィッチ] ... ¥800
   ハム・レタス・サラミ・トマト・卵他2種より
3. SAINTS. PÉRES SANDWICH [VEGETA] [サンペール サンドウィッチ] ... ¥800
   アボカド・チェダーチーズ・トマト・野菜2種より
4. CASSE-CROÛTE [カスクルート] ¥700
   バゲットにハム、サラミ、レタス、トマト、クリームチーズ他
5. SMOKED SALMON [スモークサーモン] ¥1,000
   スモークサーモンとバター・チーズ・玉ねぎとレモン
6. STEAK-SANDWICH [ステーキサンド] ¥1,200
   ステーキサンド・フレンチマスタード
7. JAMBON [ジャンボン] ¥700
   生ハム、ガトン、玉ねぎ、ピクルス、マヨ他

【SALAD】

8. DES PRÉS SALAD [デプレサラダ] ¥700
   グリーンサラダ、バジルソース、野菜グリル他アンチョビ
9. SALAD NIÇOISE [サラダニソワーズ] ¥900
   レタス、オイル・サーディン、玉子、アンチョビ他

【SOUP】

10. CLAM CHOWDER [クラムチャウダー] ¥300

【DRINK】

1. BLEND COFFEE [ブレンドコーヒー] ¥300
2. CAFÉ AU LAIT [カフェオレ] ¥400
3. CAPPUCCINO [カプチーノ] ¥400
4. EARL GREY TEA [アールグレイティー] ¥300
5. DARJEELING TEA [ダージリンティー] ¥300
6. COCOA [ココア] ¥400
7. ICED COFFEE [アイスコーヒー] ¥300
8. ICED CAFÉ AU LAIT [アイスカフェオレ] ¥400
9. ICED TEA [アイスティー] ¥400
10. ICED COCOA [アイスココア] ¥400
11. FRESH JUICE [フレッシュジュース] ¥400

テーブル カフェ渋谷店 営業時間11:00〜20:00
渋谷区神宮前4-9-14 トゥモローランド3F TEL.03-3400-7704 FAX.03-3406-7818

FAXにてオーダー11:30以降にてお受けし、FAX.03-3406-7818
TAKE OUTで30分前にお込みください
TAKE OUT HOURS 12:00〜20:00

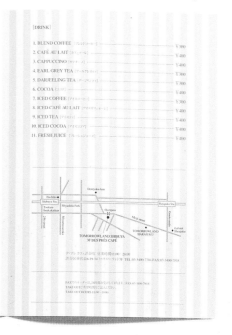

DES PRÉS CAFÉ
information

contents

デ・プレ カフェでは パーティーをさまざまや、
ティーパーティーからウェディング二次会の
パーティーまで承っております。

ご予約・お問い合わせ毎日営業時間11:00〜20:00以内までご連絡いただけます。

Telephone:03-3400-7704
Facsimile:03-3400-7818

ご予約、お問い合わせは営業時間11:00〜20:00以内までご連絡いただけます。

party

【貸切パーティー】
人数:10〜60名様
料金:¥4,000〜

[Menu Sample A]
Hors-D'oeuvre [Hot & Cold] 前菜
Assorted Cheeses チーズ盛り合わせ
Salad サラダ
Stewed Beef 牛肉の煮込み
Spaghetti "Pepenoncini" 魚介のパスタ
Desserts デザート

[Menu Sample B]
Carpaccio 牛肉のカルパッチョ
Seafood Marine 魚介のマリネ
Jambon Salad 生ハムのサラダ
Assorted Sausage ソーセージの盛り合わせ
Cold Pasta 冷たいパスタ
Grilled Salmon サーモンのグリル
Provancian Saffran-rice サフランライスのリゾット他

[Menu Sample C]
Cold Meet コールドミート
House Made Sandwiches 自家製サンドウィッチ
Omelet オムレツ
Spear Libs スペアリブ
Spear Fish Steak カジキマグロのステーキ
Pasta パスタ
Fried Rice ライスのピラフ他

ご予約のキャンセルは12日前に承ります。なお当日のキャンセル料は
お申し出ください。

private party

パーティデパーティー、
ティーパーティーなどいかがですか。

【プライベートパーティー】
人数:2名様〜
料金:¥2,000

[Brunch Menu]
Soup スープ
Salad サラダ
Sandwich サンドウィッチ
Sweet デザート
Soft Drink ソフトドリンク

[Tea Time Menu]
Open Sandwich オープンサンドウィッチ
Fruit フルーツ
Cake ケーキ
Soft Drink ソフトドリンク

[Sun Set Menu]
Aperatif アペリティフ
Hors D'oeuvre 前菜
Pasta パスタ
Desart デザート
Soft Drink ソフトドリンク

DES PRÉS CAFÉ

DES PRÉS CAFÉ [SHIBUYA]
3F TOMORROWLAND 4-9-14 JINGUMAE SHIBUYA-KU TOKYO
TEL.03-3400-7704 FAX.03-3406-7818
OPEN 11:00〜20:00

パリのカフェをイメージしてストライプ模様を様々なシーンで使用。カフェはグリーン、パン屋はブラウンという風にコーナーにより色分けし、ストライプ模様を、店のテント部分とグラフィックスにおとしこみ、統一感を出している。

A stripe motif applied to a variety of scenes supports the Paris café image. Color changes — green for the café, brown for the bakery — differentiate the sections. Extending the different stripe patterns to the awnings and graphics creates a sense of unity.

マコーズ・ベーグル・カフェ
MACOU'S BAGEL CAFE　Japan
東京都目黒区東山4-1-1 風見ビル1F
1F Kazami-Bldg., 4-1-1 Higashiyama Meguro-ku Tokyo

A： 田井 裕　Yutaka Tai
AF： ㈱フレスコ　Design Fresco
CD, AD, D, I： 柳沢高文　Takafumi Yanagisawa
P： 馬場良門　Yoshikado Baba
CW： 木村祐子　Yuko Kimura
DF： 柳沢広告制作室
　　　Yanagisawa Advertising Creative Room

東京にいながらニューヨーク気分を味わえる店内では、
手作りのベーグルと香ばしいコーヒーを毎日楽しめる。
グラフィックデザインも、手作りのぬくもりを大切にした店
のイメージと統一感を持たせて温かい仕上がりにしている。

A taste of New York—home of the bagel—in Tokyo. The sense
of warmth this store offering home-baked bagels and fresh-
brewed coffee projects, is expressed in the graphic design as well.

ベーグル アンド ベーグル　BAGEL & BAGEL　Japan
東京都港区六本木7-3-13 秋山ビル1F
1F Akiyama-Bldg., 7-3-13 Roppongi Minato-ku Tokyo

A： 白崎 裕 Hiroshi Shirasaki
AF： エー アール エス設計事務所 ARS Architects

ショップカード　Shop Card

ポストカード　Post Card

日本人にはまだなじみの少なかったベーグルを、いち早く
紹介したベーグルの専門店。「シンプル＆ナチュラル」
「老若男女を選ばない店づくり」をキーワードに、ファース
トフード店ではなくクイックサービスレストランを目指す。

The first specialty store to introduce yet unfamiliar bagels to
Japan. Imaged to be "simple and natural" and "appeal to
people of all ages," the shop aims to make inroads not as a
fast-food but rather as a fast-service shop.

Bagels

ラ・プレッツェル La Pretzel Japan

東京都渋谷区神宮前4-31-11 コスモ原宿1-2F
1-2F Cosmo Harajuku, 4-31-11 Jingumae Shibuya-ku Tokyo

CD: 菅井克枝 Yoshie Sugai
D: アン・ルイス Ann L. Lewis

日本ではまだ珍しいプレッツェルの専門店は、活気あふ
れる原宿という街を意識して、黄色と赤色をグラフィッ
クに配した元気のいいイメージづくりがなされている。
店内にはアーティストのアン・ルイスがデザインしたプ
レッツェルのオブジェが飾られている。

Still a rarity in Japan, this pretzel shop plays off of the
exuberance of the Harajuku area with its high-spirited yellow
and red trademark store image. A pretzel sculpture by artist
Ann Lewis is exhibited inside.

アジアン・バーガー　ASIAN BURGER　Japan

東京都渋谷区神宮前4-29-8
4-29-8 Jingumae Shibuya-ku Tokyo

A：辻中浩佑　Hiroyuki Tsujinaka
AF：ワックス・トラックス　Wax Trax
CD：長谷川康之　Yasuyuki Hasegawa
AD：田川雅一　Masakazu Tagawa
D：小野達也　Tatsuya Ono

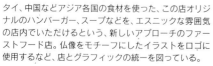

タイ、中国などアジア各国の食材を使った、この店オリジナルのハンバーガー、スープなどを、エスニックな雰囲気の店内でいただけるという、新しいアプローチのファーストフード店。仏像をモチーフにしたイラストをロゴに使用するなど、店とグラフィックの統一を図っている。

A new approach to the fast food restaurant — original recipe hamburgers and soups using ingredients from Thai, Chinese and other East Asian cuisine served in an ethic environment. The Buddha motif used in the logo enhances the Oriental atmosphere.

ティンブクトゥ TIMBUKTUU USA

841 42nd Street, Des Moines, Iowa 50312

AF：ディーシーエム・グループ DCM Group
CD, AD, D, I：ジョン・セイルズ John Sayles
DF：セイルズ・グラフィック・デザイン
Sayles Graphic Design

一連のグラフィックモチーフ上に展開されている、温かみの
あるアーストーンのインクと紙の色そして手書き文字が、オ
フビートで素朴ではあるが上品な印象を与えている。アー
ストーンと土着のモチーフはインテリアの壁面、コーヒー
カップ、ナプキン、そして建物の構造材をも飾っている。

Timbuktuu Coffee Bars' collateral material revolves around a
series of graphic images. Warm earth-tone ink and paper colors
and hand-rendered type add an offbeat, rustic-but-refined
touch. Earth tones and native imagery are also boldly applied in
the interior design, to wall murals, coffee cups, napkins, and
structural elements of the building.

ジャンバ・ジュース　jamba juice　USA

AD, D： ジャック・アンダーソン　Jack Anderson
D： リサ・サービニィ　Lisa Cerveny
スザンヌ・ハドン　Suzanne Haddon
ソニア・マックス　Sonja Max
ヘイディ・フェイバー　Heidi Favour
クリフ・チュン　Cliff Chung
I： ミツ・カタヤマ　Mits Katayama
CW： スーキィ・ハットン　Suky Hutton
DF： ホーナル・アンダーソン・デザイン・ワークス
Hornall Anderson Design Works, Inc.

「コップの中の食事」として知られているジャンバ・ジュースは、ジュースによる栄養補給という特徴を持っており、『ジャンバ・ジュース』を他の競合するファーストフードと区別することを目的に、ロゴとグラフィックのデザインがなされている。

A logotype and kit-of-parts designed to distinguish Jamba Juice from its competition in fast-food alternatives. The identity needed to communicate that Jamba Juice is the authority on juice and nutrition, or as they describe it--"a meal in a cup." It needed to look fresh and festive, but not too trendy.

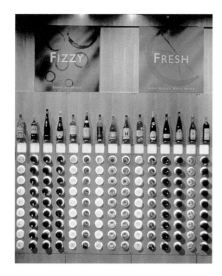

ベスト・セラーズ　BEST CELLARS　USA

AF： ロックウェル・グループ　Rockwell Group
AD, D： ジャック・アンダーソン　Jack Anderson
　　D： リサ・サービニィ　Lisa Cerveny
　　　　デビッド・ベイツ　David Bates
　D, I： ジャナ・ウィルソン・エセール　Jana Wilson Esser
　　　I： ニコール・ブロス　Nicole Bloss
　　　P： ポール・ウォーショル　Paul Warchol
　　DF： ホーナル・アンダーソン・デザイン・ワークス
　　　　Hornall Anderson Design Works, Inc.

赤ワインのボトルがテーブルクロスに残すワインのシミ
の環をモチーフとし、そのワインのシミの形をデザイン
に取り込んだ一連の隠喩的シンボルが、8種に分類され
たワインのそれぞれを表している。ミニマルなイメージ
が、評判を落とすことなく手ごろさを伝えている。

A minimalist presentation conveys affordability without compromising
taste. This unpretentious identity is built on a wine stain motif — the
characteristic ring a red wine bottle frequently leaves on tablecloths.
A series of metaphoric icons, also developed using the basic wine
stain shape, identify the eight categories of wine.

クラトッホヴィル　KRATOCHWILL　Slovenia

Kolodvorska 5, 1000 Ljubljana

A：ミリャーナ・ネデリコビッチ・ベルセッチ
　　　Mirjana Nedeljkovič Berčič
AD, D：エディ・バーク　Edi Berk
P：ジャネッツ・パクセッチ　Janez Pukšič
DF：ケーログ　KROG

クラトッホヴィルは新しいブリュワリー兼パブ。自家製
のビールとスロベニアの伝統料理を楽しめる。伝統的スタイルのロゴマークは、200年の歴史をもったブリュワリーというストーリーのためにデザインされている。

Kratochwill is a new brewery and pub serving homemade beer and traditional Slovenian cuisine. The traditional-style logomark is designed to give the impression the brewery has a 200-year history.

プリ・ククリュ　Pri Kuklju　Slovenia
Velike Lašče 18, 1315 Velike Lašče

AD, D：エディ・バーク　Edi Berk
　P：ジャネッツ・パクセッチ　Janez Pukšič
　DF：ケーログ　KROG

1778年以来、地域の料理をつくりつづけてきた
伝統的スロベニアン・スタイルのレストラン。イン
テリアには222年前の建物の壁とすすで黒ずんだ
厨房が取り入れられている。

A traditional Slovenian-style restaurant serving
regional cooking since 1778. The restaurant interior
incorporates an original wall from the 222-year-old
building, and the "black (soot-stained) kitchen."

メニュー　Menu

187

アルト・スタツィオーネ　ALT Stazione　Germany

CD： コンラッド・ウィンザー　Conrad Winzer
AD： ジャン=ベノア・レヴィ　Jean-Benoît Levy
AD, D： ハイネル・ショーフェルベルガー　Heiner Schaufelberger
P： ダニエル・スペア　Daniel Spehr
DF： アンド（トラフィック・グラフィック）And (Trafic Grafic)

ランチョンマット　Luncheon Mat

ポストカード　Post Card

伝票　Bill

コースター
Coaster

ショップカード
Shop Card

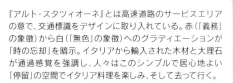

『アルト・スタツィオーネ』とは高速道路のサービスエリア
の意で、交通標識をデザインに取り入れている。赤（「義務」
の象徴）から白（「無色」の象徴）へのグラディエーションが
「時の忘却」を暗示。イタリアから輸入された木材と大理石
が通過感覚を強調し、人々はこのシンプルで居心地よい
「停留」の空間でイタリア料理を楽しみ、そして去って行く。

Alt Stazione means "highway stop," hence the traffic sign. The
red (symbolizing "obligation") to white ("colorlessness")
gradation suggests "forgetting time." Woods and marble
imported from Italy support the sense of transit. A simple, cozy
"stop" at which to eat — Italian food — and go.

ピュートニー・ブリッジ・レストラン
Putney Blidge Restaurant UK
1, Embankment, Putney, London SW151LB

AF：バスキン・キリアキデス・サンズ Paskin Kyriakides Sands

メニュー Menu

ショップカード Shop Card

南西フランスの影響を受けたモダンフランス料理を、コクのある香りと最高級の食材を使用して提案。この建物はロンドンで最高のレストランからの眺めにスタイリッシュでモダンな機能的背景を添えている。レストランの全テーブルはテムズ川を見渡す眺望を備えている。

Modern French cuisine with influences from southwest France, using robust flavors and the highest quality ingredients. The building provides a stylish, modern and functional backdrop to one of London's finest restaurant views; it is designed such that all tables in the restaurant have panoramic views across the Thames.

クロスオーバー crossover Italy

Lungomare Tintori, Rimini 47900

A, AF：ロベルタ・マルツィ Roberta Marzi
CD, AD, D：ステファノ・トンティ Stefano Tonti
DF：ステファノ・トンティ・デザイン Stefano Tonti Design

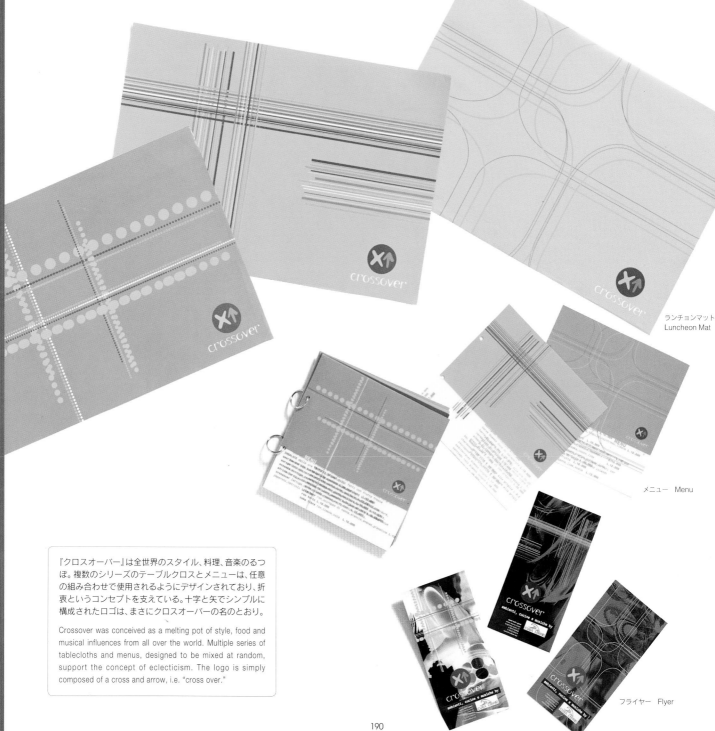

ランチョンマット
Luncheon Mat

メニュー Menu

フライヤー Flyer

『クロスオーバー』は全世界のスタイル、料理、音楽のるつ
ぼ。複数のシリーズのテーブルクロスとメニューは、任意
の組み合わせで使用されるようにデザインされており、折
衷というコンセプトを支えている。十字と矢でシンプルに
構成されたロゴは、まさにクロスオーバーの名のとおり。

Crossover was conceived as a melting pot of style, food and
musical influences from all over the world. Multiple series of
tablecloths and menus, designed to be mixed at random,
support the concept of eclecticism. The logo is simply
composed of a cross and arrow, i.e. "cross over."

グローブ　THE GLOBE USA

373 Park Avenue South, New York, NY 10010

A：ジェームス・ビーバー　James Biber
　　マイケル・ツベック・ブロンナー　Michael Zweck-Bronner
D：ジム・ブラウン　Jim Brown
　　ポーラ・シェア　Paula Scher
　　キース・ダイグル　Keith Daigle
AF, DF：ペンタグラム　Pentagram

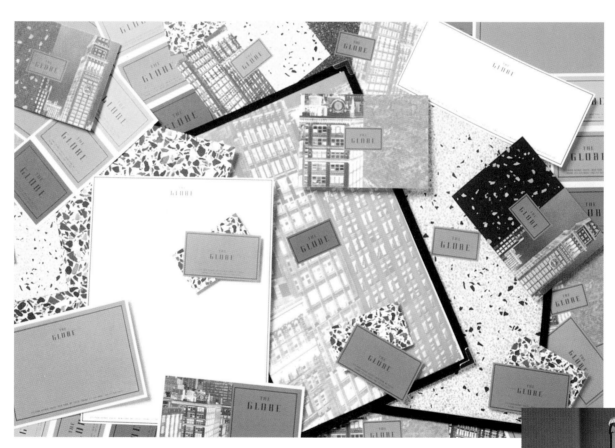

20世紀初めのアメリカン・カフェテリアにあったカジュアルな雰囲気と広さを気軽に手本とした店内は、優雅で清潔なイメージ。料理は異国的というよりは懐かしさを感じさせ、インテリアデザインは「以前訪れたことのあるような新しい場所」というコンセプトに基づき、クラシックな材料から新しい使い方を引き出している。

Loosely based on the scale and casual atmosphere of the early 20th-century American cafeteria, Glove is both elegant and sanitary in image, with food more familiar than exotic. The interior design plays off the referential aspect of the concept: a new place you have been before. The materials are classic, their uses are new.

ケンズ デリ＆カフェ
Ken's DeLI & CaFe Japan
東京都新宿区新宿3-26-6 FFビル1F, B1F
B1F-1F FF-Bldg., 3-26-6 Shinjuku Shinjuku-ku Tokyo

CD： 井上盛夫　Morio Inoue
AD, D： 飯島広昭　Hiroaki Iijima
DF： 北山創造研究所
　　　Kitayama & Company Visual Planning & Design
　　　ちゃんとフードサービス
　　　Chanto Food Service Inc.

「ヨーロッパにある日本食のデリ＆カフェ」をイメージしたこの店は、照明をうまく使った陰影の空間演出が印象的。店が掲げる「日本から世界へ」というコンセプトを、ロゴマークに用いた「火焔」で表現している。

Imaged as a Japanese deli/café in Europe, skillful use of lighting creates a dramatic spatial effect with light and shadow. The concept "from Japan to the world" the shop upholds is expressed by the flame in the logomark.

COLDS

HOTS

KEN'S ONIGIRI

エニィタイム　anytime　China

1/F JP Plaza, 22-36 Paterson Street, Causeway Bay, Hong Kong

A：ヘルナン・A・ザンゲリーニ　Hernan A. Zanghellini
AF：ザンゲリーニ・ホルト・アーキテクツ
　　 Zanghellini Holt Architects
CD, AD, D：アラン・チャン　Alan Chan
D：ポリー・コー　Polly Ko / ミウ・チョイ　Miu Choy
DF：アラン・チャン・デザイン　Alan Chan Design Co.

カジュアルな雰囲気で香港とアジアの料理を提供。「エニィ
タイム」の名が表すように、ブレックファースト、ランチ、
ディナーを客の好きな時に楽しんでもらうよう、一日を通し
同メニューを扱っている。ロゴの中の数字9-2-4-7-1-0-3-2
にはこのユニークなカフェの個性が表われている。

A contemporary environment with a casual atmosphere serving
authentic Hong Kong and Asian food. As the name "Anytime"
implies, the same menu offered throughout the day allows
customers to enjoy breakfast, lunch and dinner anytime they
please. The numbers 9-2-4-7-1-0-3-2 in the logotype reflect the
true personality of this unique café.

コースター　Coaster

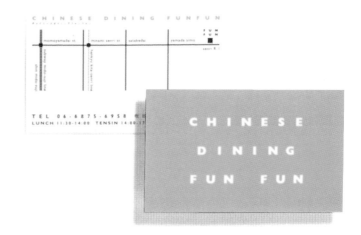

チャイニーズ ダイニング ファンファン
CHINESE DINING FUN FUN　Japan
大阪府吹田市山田西1-36-3
1-36-3 Yamada-nishi Suita-shi Osaka

　A, CD：大月勝弘　Katsuhiro Otsuki
　　　D：松原 香　Kaori Matsubara
　　　P：ナカサ アンド パートナーズ　Nacása & Partners Inc.
AF, DF：㈱ケー・ディー　K. D Inc.

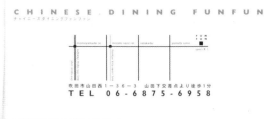

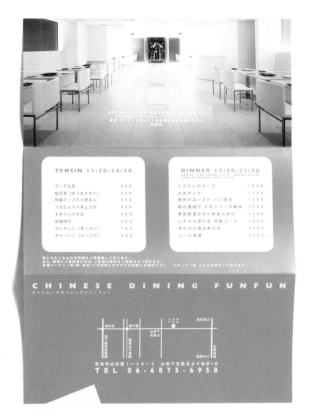

メニュー　Menu

従来の中国料理店のイメージを覆すスタイリッシュな空間デザインが印象的。白とオレンジのショップカラーと店名を強く印象づけられるよう、店舗とグラフィックツールのデザインを連動させている。

Stylish space design dispels the conventional Chinese restaurant image. Orange and white as used in the store and logo create a strong impression; store design and graphic tools work in tandem.

ソーホーズ　SOHO'S　Japan

東京都渋谷区宇田川町14-14 Kビル 1-2F
1-2F K-Bldg., 14-14 Udagawa-cho Shibuya-ku Tokyo

AF：ファイブワン設計事務所　Five One
A：田口 勇　Isamu Taguchi
Planner：月川蘇豊　Soho Tsukikawa
CD：八木正人　Masato Yagi
AD：瀬川浩樹　Hiroki Segawa
D：相川一明　Kazuaki Aikawa
CW：御倉直文　Naofumi Onkura (1)
DF：㈱電通　Dentsu Inc.

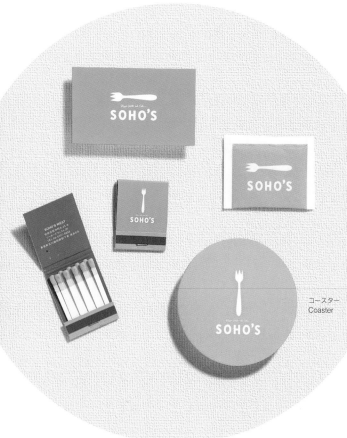

コースター
Coaster

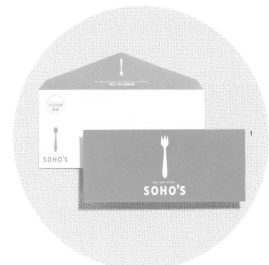

清潔感いっぱいの白タイルの外壁。大きな窓から差し込む太陽の光。その明るいイメージを反映させたグラフィックデザイン。まるでカリフォルニアにあるレストランのような店内では、薪で焼くピザなど、季節感あふれるカジュアルなイタリア料理を楽しめる。

Clean, white exterior walls. Sunlight streaming in through a large window. Pizza baked in a wood-burning oven and other seasonal, informal Italian dishes served in an atmosphere that feels like California. The graphics reflect the same bright image.

メニュー　Menu

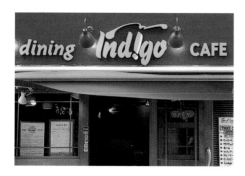

ダイニング カフェ インディゴ
dining CAFE Ind!go　Japan

東京都港区南青山2-22-1
2-22-1 Minami-Aoyama Minato-ku Tokyo

AF： ㈱エー・アンド・ティー　A&T
DF： ㈱パシオ　Pasio

コースター
Coaster

イタリアンをベースにした創作料理を提供するダイニングカフェ。店名になっている「indigo」（藍色の意味）を店のいたる所に使用し、全体的にさわやかなイメージを意識した演出になっている。

A dining café offering Italian-based original cuisine. In keeping with the name, indigo is used throughout the store interior as well as in the graphics, which creates a fresh overall image.

カフェ・ラ・フォルケッタ　caffe la forchetta　Japan

福岡県福岡市博多区中洲4-6-12
4-6-12 Nakasu Hakata-ku Fukuoka-shi Fukuoka

A：勝野明正　Akimasa Katsuno
AF：ケイズデザイン　K's Design
AD, D：國松義生　Yoshio Kunimatsu
P：知識たかし　Takashi Chishiki
Stylist：中村ゆり子　Yuriko Nakamura（1）
I：土器修三　Shuzo Doki
CW：岡部はち郎　Hachiro Okabe
DF：㈱九十九島エスケイファーム
Kujyukushima Esukei Firm Co., Ltd.

メニュー　Menu

ニューヨーク・スタイルのイタリアンレストラン＆カフェ。グラフィック類も、ニューヨーク・スタイルをコンセプトに、シンプルで分かりやすいデザインになっている。店名はイタリア語で「フォーク」の意味。

Simple, straight forward graphics support the image of a New York-style Italian restaurant and café. The name means "fork" in Italian.

INFORMATION

Makeup Room

Italian Style

in Dining

WEDDING

CAFFE LA FORCHETTA

La tavola in caffe la forchetta

PASTA

Pasta al pesto di basilico

CUCINA

Scorfano alla Mediterranea

SALUTE!

caffe la
forchetta
ristorante

Chardonnay

VINO

Pizza margherita

PIZZA

Panna cotta con tapioca

DOLCE

La tavola in caffe la forch

caffe la forchetta
Grand Open

ル·プティ·ブドン　Le Petit Bedon　Japan

東京都渋谷区鉢山町13-13 ヒルサイドウエストA
Hillside West-A, 13-13 Hachiyama-cho Shibuya-ku Tokyo

A ： 杉 千春　Chiharu Sugi
　　高橋真奈美　Manami Takahashi
　　藤江和子　Kazuko Fujie
AF： プラネットワークス　Planet Works Co., Ltd.
　　藤江和子アトリエ　Kazuko Fujie Atelier

ショップカード　Shop Card

フランス語で「小太鼓腹」を意味する名のこの店は、フランスのワインカーヴをイメージしたレストランが地下に、モダンなイメージのカフェが1Fにあり、フランス人の客でにぎわっている。店名からイメージされたおじさんのイラストロゴが親しみを感じさせる。

A basement restaurant imaged after a French wine cellar with a modern-looking café on the ground floor bustles with French clientele. The middle-aged man illustration/logo used with the restaurant name—"little beer-belly" in French—exudes a friendly feeling.

マヌビッシュ mannebiches Japan
東京都文京区根津1-16-8
1-16-8 Nezu Bunkyo-ku Tokyo

A： 永島博文 Hirobumi Nagashima
AF： ㈱テトラ Te.t.o.ra
AD, D： 末広峰治 Mineji Suehiro
DF： パワーデザイン Power Design

ポストカード
Post Card

伝票 Bill

「親しい人とくつろぎながら自然の恵みを楽しむ店」をコンセプトに、地中海地方に受け継がれる家庭料理を日本流にアレンジした料理が並ぶ。陽気な雰囲気あふれる明るいレストラン。

Mediterranean home cooking rearranged Japanese style offered in a bright and cheery atmosphere designed as "a place to relax with intimate friends and enjoy the blessings of nature."

ラ・クロッシュ
LA CLOCHE　Japan
大阪府大阪市中央区北浜3-1-18
3-1-18 Kitahama Chuo-ku Osaka-shi Osaka

A：佐藤史仁　Fumihito Sato
AF：コンプレックス　Complex
AD：立花幹也　Mikiya Tachibana
DF：イエロー ドッグ スタジオ　Yellow Dog Studio

料理、空間、サービスの総合力で、顧客を包み込むフレンチ・レストラン。そのヒューマンサイズの温かさを、ドラマチックな空間とグラフィックデザインで表現している。

A French restaurant that embraces customers with the combined power of cuisine, atmosphere, and service. The warmth of its human scale is expressed in the dramatic space and graphic design.

日本の料理 ロイス ジェイ スタイル
LOIS j STYLE　Japan
大阪府大阪市北区茶屋町19-19
19-19 Chaya-machi Kita-ku Osaka-shi Osaka

　A：佐藤史仁　Fumihito Sato
AF：コンプレックス　Complex
AD：立花幹也　Mikiya Tachibana
　I：井川友晴　Tomoharu Ikawa
CW：矢野桂志　Keiji Yano
DF：イエロー ドッグ スタジオ　Yellow Dog Studio

コースター　Coaster

フライヤー　Flyer

ショップカード
Shop Card

「和」の本質をいまの感覚でとらえたコンテンポラリーな和食レストラン。凛とした緊張感と、心落ち着かせる優しさがとけあうような「ダイナミズムと静のコントラスト」が、デザインのコンセプトになっている。

A Japanese restaurant that captures the essence of wa (Japanese spirit) in a contemporary rendition. The design concept expresses "the contrast between dynamism and serenity" blending a dignified tension with a relaxing gentleness.

茶語 アラン·チャン ティールーム
「Cha Yǔ」Alan Chan Tea Room　Japan

東京都渋谷区千駄ヶ谷5-24-2 新宿高島屋6F
6F Shinjuku Takashimaya, 5-24-2 Sendagaya Shibuya-ku Tokyo

A, CD, AD, D : アラン·チャン　Alan Chan
　　　　AF : ㈱ジアス·アソシエイツ
　　　　　　 The Earth Associates Co., Ltd.
　　　　DF : アラン·チャン デザイン　Alan Chan Design Co.

コースター　Coaster

206

世界で活躍する香港のグラフィックデザイナー、アラン・チャンのプロデュースにより、「西洋と東洋の融合」をコンセプトにショップデザインされたカフェ。中国茶をはじめ世界のお茶と各国の料理をアレンジしたオリジナルメニューを提供している。

A café based on the concept "the fusion of East and West" produced by internationally active Hong Kong graphic designer Alan Chan. The menu offers teas of the world and originally arranged international dishes.

丸の内カフェ　MARUNOUCHI CAFE　Japan
東京都千代田区丸の内3-2-3 フジビル1F
1F Fuji Bldg., 3-2-3 Marunouchi, Chiyoda-ku Tokyo

Interior Designer : ウォン・キン・ホー　Wong Kin Ho
　　　　　AF : エムイーシー・デザイン・インターナショナル
　　　　　　　 MEC Design International Corp.
　CD, AD, D : アラン・チャン　Alan Chan
　　　　　　D : ピーター・ロー　Peter Lo
　　　　　DF : アラン・チャン・デザイン
　　　　　　　 Alan Chan Design Co.

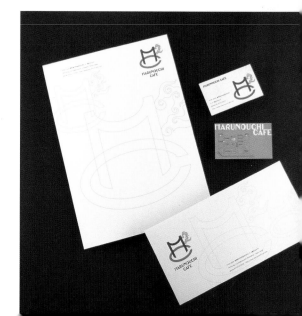

ビジネスセンター内のオアシスとして創られた、ヴァーチャ
ル・カフェ。ギャラリー、IT、宣伝、自動販売機、リラクゼー
ションのスペースより構成されている。中国と東南アジアか
ら輸入されたアンティーク家具はそれぞれのスペースを結び
付け、空間に人間味を与えている。

A virtual café — conceived as an oasis within a business center —
comprised of gallery, IT, promotional, vending machine, and
relaxation areas.　Antique furniture imported from China and
Southeast Asia links the spaces and adds a touch of humanity.

福多多　Fu duo duo　China

Shop 7C, G/F, Site 1, Whampoa Garden, Hunghom,
Kowloon, Hong Kong

    A : キミー・チャン　Kimmy Chan
CD, AD : カン・タイ・クン　Kan Tai-Keung
AD, D, I : エディ・ユー・チー・コン　Eddy Yu Chi Kong
    D : ラム・ワイ・フン　Lam Wai Hung
    P : シー・ケー・ウォン　C. K. Wong
    I : ステファン・ラウ　Stephen Lau
    DF : カン＆ラウ デザイン・コンサルタンツ
        Kan & Lau Design Consultants

オーナーの顔を楽しく幸せそうにマンガ化し、視覚的に特
徴づけた地方のレストラン。この楽しさいっぱいのレスト
ランは『福多多』と名付けられ、自由奔放な書体はこのレス
トランの親しみやすい雰囲気と料理の質を表している。

A local restaurant with a visual identity featuring a jolly and
contented cartoon rendition of the proprietor. The fun-filled
restaurant name, (literally "lots and lots of luck"), and its free-
style typography reflect the restaurant's friendly atmosphere
and quality food.

青龍門ウエスト　SEIRYUMON WEST　Japan

東京都世田谷区中町5-25-9 ソーホーズ ウエスト B1F
B1F Soho's West-Bldg., 5-25-9 Naka-machi Setagaya-ku Tokyo

A：鈴木恵千代　Shigechiyo Suzuki
AF：㈱乃村工藝社　Nomura Co., Ltd.
Planner：月川蘇豊　Soho Tsukikawa
Planner, D：李 泰栄　Tae-Young Lee (1)
D：田尻好範　Yoshinori Tajiri
DF：㈱ももプラン　Momo Plans Inc. (1)
　オフィス ドゥーイング　Office Doing

メニュー Menu

リーフレット
Leaflet

ビルに挟まれて立ち退きを迫られている古い民家をイメージした
外観の台湾家庭小皿料理店。店内は東洋と西洋が、そして過去
と未来が融合した食の異次元空間を意識し、アジアの喧騒と
エネルギーを表現した、壁一面のオリジナルパチンコ台は圧巻。

A home-style Taiwanese dim sum restaurant with an exterior
patterned after the old, indigenous houses that are gradually losing
ground to high-rise buildings. Inside, a fusion of Oriental and
Occidental, old and new creates another dining dimension,
expressing Asian bustle and energy. The original pachinko machine
wall mural is a knockout.

アジアンダイニング 汎
ASIAN DINING FAN Japan

東京都渋谷区宇田川町13-16 コクサイビルA館2F
2F Kokusai-Bldg.-A, 13-16 Udagawa-cho
Shibuya-ku Tokyo

A： 平井真臣 Masaomi Hirai
AF： ㈱エイム クリエイツ Aim Creats Co., Ltd.

コースター Coaster

インドネシアのリゾート、バリ島をイメージした店内の随所に、現地の伝統的工芸品を配置し、リゾート地のような開放感を味わえるようテラス席も設けてある。渋谷にいながらアジア情緒を味わえる空間。

Imaged after an Indonesian resort on the island of Bali, with traditional handicrafts displayed at every turn, and terrace seating that has a resort-like the sense of openness. The space offers a taste of Southeast Asia in the heart of Shibuya.

一風亭 Ippu-tei Japan

岡山県岡山市津島南1-1-27
1-1-27 Tsushima-minami Okayama-shi Okayama

A： 高田康久 Yasuhisa Takada
橋本泰久 Yasuhisa Hashimoto
AF： 誠屋工務店 Makoto-ya Building Co.
CD, CW： 妹尾雅昭 Masaaki Seno
AD, D, I： 橋本和尚 Yasuhisa Hashimoto
P： 岡田祐司 Yuji Okada
DF： ハシモトグラフィック事務所
Hashimoto Graphic Office

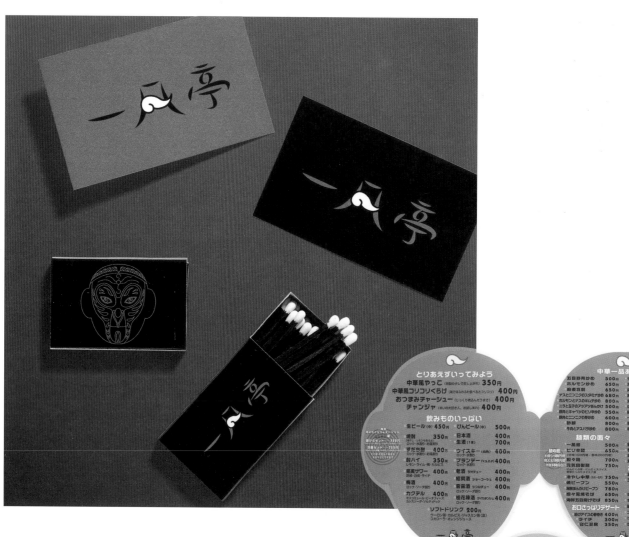

以前はまったく目立たない中華風居酒屋だった店を、目
立つこと、中華のイメージを明確に打ち出して新しい客
を確保することをコンセプトに、リニューアルオープン。
京劇風のイラストを取り入れたメニューや店名ロゴな
ど、グラフィックデザインが際立っている。

A Chinese pub that previously went unnoticed renewed its
image emphasizing the following criteria: stand out, have a
distinctly Chinese image, and secure new customers. The
Chinese Opera illustration used in the logo and menu is
striking.

シャンゼリ～ゼ キリン
CHAMPS ÉLYSÉES KIRIN　Japan

大阪府大阪市西区新町1-29-10 平和相互ビル1F
1F Heiwasogo-Bldg., 1-29-10 Shin-machi Nishi-ku
Osaka-shi Osaka

A :	山田剛志 Tsuyoshi Yamada
CD, AD :	金山正一 Shoichi Kanayama
D :	中井由美子 Yumiko Nakai
AF, DF :	㈱ボーイ・カンパニー Boy Company, Ltd.

ポストカード　Post Card

個性的なこのバーの店名は、パリのシャンゼリゼ通りに
雰囲気が似た通りが店の前にあり、さらにオーナーがキ
リンに似ているところからついた。店内はパリの街で捕
らえられた檻の中にいるキリンのイメージ。ロゴになっ
ているイラストはオーナーの似顔絵である。

The unique name of this bar derives from the fact that the
street it faces resembles Champs-Elysees and the owner
looks like a giraffe. The interior is imaged after a giraffe in a
cage caught on the streets of Paris. The illustration in the
logo is a caricature of the owner.

コースター
Coaster

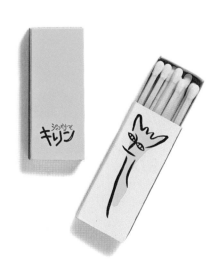

213

ブラーボ キリン　BRAVO KIRIN　Japan

大阪府大阪市中央区東心斎橋1-9-12
1-9-12 Higashi-Shinsaibashi Chuo-ku Osaka-shi Osaka

A, CD, AD：金山正一　Shoichi Kanayama
　　　　D：富永君子　Kimiko Tominaga
　　　　 I：池田味嘉子　Mikako Ikeda
AF, DF：㈱ボーイ・カンパニー　Boy Company, Ltd.

ポストカード　Post Card

フライヤー　Flyer

縦に長いビルが、キリンの首をイメージさせるレストラ
ン＆バー。グラフィックにもキリンの体の色を連想させ
る土っぽいカラーを取り入れ、店内は「アフリカのサフ
ァリ」を表現するため、各フロアをそれぞれ違った雰囲気
に仕上げている。

A long, narrow building augments the giraffe-neck image of
this bar and restaurant. Earth-tone colors, suggestive of a
giraffe's coloration, are adopted in the graphics. The
atmosphere varies floor-to-floor to express an African safari.

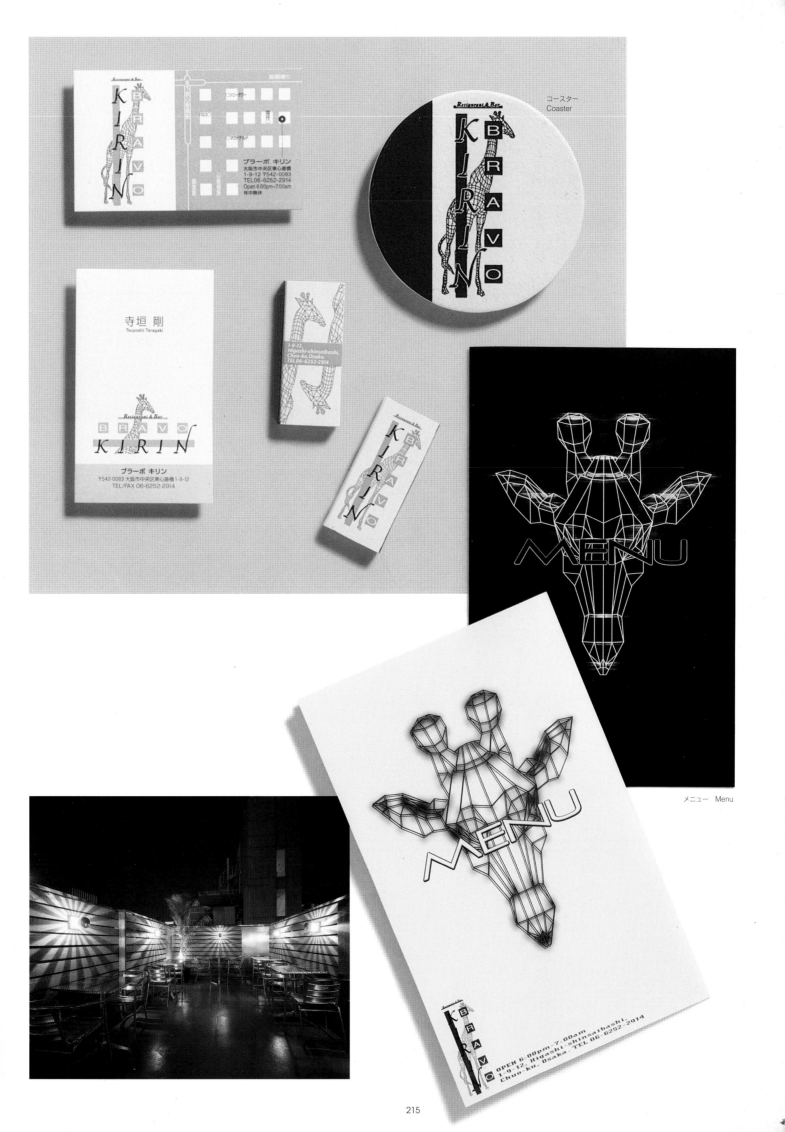

コースター
Coaster

メニュー Menu

ギンザ 十石　GINZA "Jukkoku"　Japan
東京都中央区銀座3-9-2
3-9-2 Ginza Chuo-ku Tokyo

A：高橋英昭　Hideaki Takahashi
AF：㈱ダイイチ　Dai-ichi Co., Ltd.
CD, AD, D, CW：石黒真三　Shinzo Ishiguro
Seal Carver（篆刻）：佐藤隆介　Ryusuke Sato

従来の民芸風おむすび店と異なり、「モダン和風」を基本
イメージとして店舗とグラフィックツールをデザイン。
日本古来のファーストフードであるおむすびを近代的な
感覚で提供し、また贈答品としても使えるよう、高級感
と清潔感を大切にしている。

In a departure from the folkcraft look of conventional rice ball
shops, "Japanese modern" forms the basis for the interior and
graphic design of a store offering a contemporary approach to
this time-honored Japanese fast food. The added sense of
quality and cleanliness make the product a viable gift item.

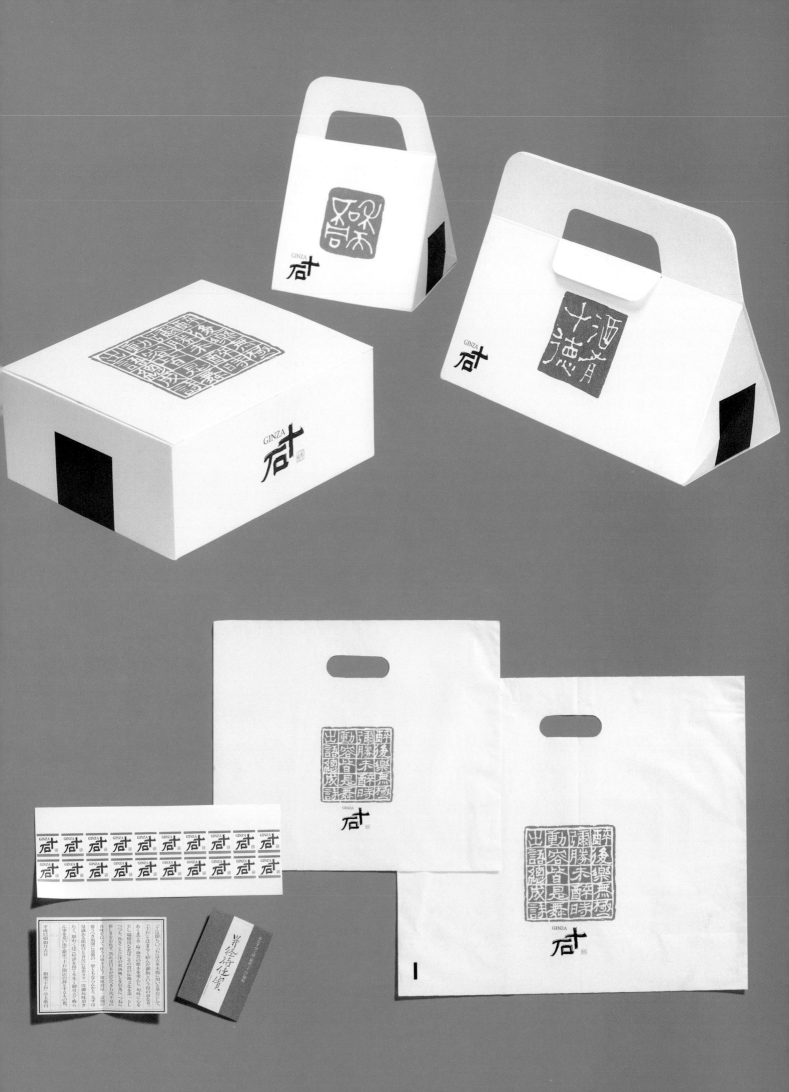

福光屋　SAKE SHOP FUKUMITSUYA　Japan

東京都中央区銀座5-5-8-1F
1F, 5-5-8 Ginza Chuo-ku Tokyo

A：植木莞爾　Kanji Ueki
AF：カサッポ＆アソシエイツ　Casappo & Associates
LD：粟辻美早　Misa Awatsuji
D：中田 誠　Makoto Nakata
D：粟辻美早　Misa Awatsuji（1）
P：中道 淳（ナカサ アンド パートナーズ）
　　Jun Nakamichi (Nacása & Partners Inc.)

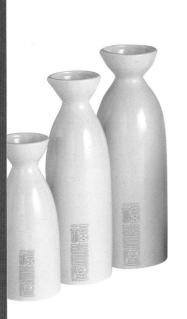

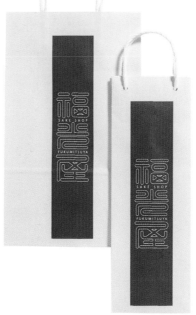

クリーンでシンプルな店内が、日本酒の透明感やボトルデザインの美しさを際立たせている。酒蔵のアンテナショップとしての機能だけではなく、日本酒の従来のイメージを打ち破り、日本酒文化全体を変えていくべく志しを持った酒屋。

A simple clean store interior sets off the beauty of sake's transparency and its richly-varied bottle design. Not satisfied to be a mere antenna shop to a sake brewery, this liquor shop shatters the conventional image of sake in an attempt to change sake culture overall.

瑞秀　SAKE CUISINE MIZUHO　Japan

東京都中央区銀座5-5-8-2F
2F, 5-5-8 Ginza Chuo-ku Tokyo

A： 植木莞爾　Kanji Ueki
AF： カサッポ＆アソシエイツ　Casappo & Associates
LD： 粟辻美早　Misa Awatsuji
D： 中田 誠　Makoto Nakata
P： 中道 淳 （ナカサ アンド パートナーズ）
　　Jun Nakamichi (Nacása & Partners Inc.)

ポストカード　Post Card

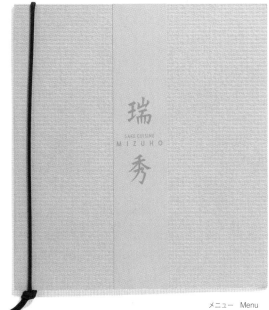

メニュー　Menu

酒屋『福光屋』の2Fにある、日本酒を中心に据えたメニューを提案する和食レストラン。国際基準を持つ日本酒をより一層おいしくいただける飲み方や、料理との組み合わせを、洗練された空間の中で体験し味わうことができる。

A Japanese restaurant on the second floor of the liquor shop Fukumitsuya offering a menu that revolves around sake. World class sake served as it should ideally be experienced, coupled with the foods that suit it best.

蓮魚　BAR Rengyo　Japan
東京都新宿区新宿3-31-1 NREビル7F
7F NRE-Bldg., 3-31-1 Shinjuku Shinjuku-ku
Tokyo

AF：㈲大浦比呂志 創作デザイン研究所
　　Hiroshi Oura Design Office
CD：飯田進悟　Singo Iida
AD：矢幡耕一　Koichi Yahata
　D：渡辺智美　Tomomi Watanabe
　　立石佳代　Kayo Tatsuishi
DF：㈱ヘルメス　Hermes Inc.

コースター　Coaster

高級感のある和風バーを表現するため、全体的にシンプル
で落ち着きのある色をグラフィックツールに使用。また、
和風テイストを出すために、使用する紙は里紙を選択し、
店が持つイメージと統一感が出るよう工夫している。

Simple graphics in subdued colors express this Japanese-
style bar's sense of class. The use of Japanese paper
enhances the Japanese feeling and acts as a device for
unifying the overall image.

和風ダイニングバー 忍庭
DINING BAR SHINOBU TEI　Japan

東京都渋谷区恵比寿南1-14-10 福隆ビルB1F
B1F Fukuryu-Bldg.,
1-14-10 Ebisu-minami Shibuya-ku Tokyo

　　A：森井良幸　Yoshiyuki Morii
　　AF：㈱カフェ　Cafe Co.
Planner：原田康弘（キューブ）Yasuhiro Harada (Cube, Inc.)
　　CD：中東郁子　Fumiko Nakato
　　D：長田 亮　Akira Nagata (1)
　　　　戸塚崇爲　Takayuki Totsuka (2)
　　DF：トツカタカユキ デザイン事務所
　　　　Takayuki Totsuka Design Office (1)

1

2

趣きの異なる18の個室を持つ和風ダイニングバーの店内には、池や竹が配され、ほの暗い照明が大人の雰囲気を醸し出している。コンセプトは「大人の男女がお忍びでくつろげる店」。

Eighteen uniquely decorated private rooms, a pond, bamboo and dim lighting create a sophisticated-feeling Japanese dining bar built on the concept "a place where adults can relax incognito."

コースター　Coaster

ニューズ ダイニング
NEWS DINING Japan
東京都港区北青山3-6-26 SJビルB1F
B1F SJ-Bldg., 3-6-26 Kita-Aoyama Minato-ku Tokyo

A：清野燿聖　Yosei Kiyono
AF：㈱サンライズ ジャパン　Sunrise Japan Co., Ltd.
CD：坂本應尚　Masahisa Sakamoto
AD：矢幡耕一　Koichi Yahata
D：齋藤能史　Yoshifumi Saito
DF：㈱ヘルメス　Hermes Inc.

STARTER

オリエンタル風トマトのブルスケッタ ¥600

木の子とサクサクパイのミルフィーユ仕立て ¥1,000

自家製スモークチキンの竜田揚げ ¥850

SALAD

ジュリエンヌサラダ&チャイニーズ風肉味噌 ¥900

PASTA

キムチとベーコンのスパゲティ ¥1,000

MAIN

カジキマグロの煎餅揚げ、かつお風味のブラウンソース ¥1,500

マグロの三色ペッパーソテー、コチジャンと焦がしバターソース .. ¥1,700

牛ヒレ肉のグリル、オイスター風味のブラウンソース ¥2,400

RICE DISHES

スモークしたサーモンと梅肉のご飯 ¥700

ちりめんじゃこと高菜漬けのご飯 ¥600

カリフォルニア・キュイジーヌに、日本、アジア料理の
エッセンスを加えた創作料理を提供しているレストラン。
「火・水・木・土・空気」を表現することをコンセプトにデザ
インされた空間に身を置くことにより、非日常的な感覚
を味わえる店。

A restaurant offering an original form of California cuisine with
a Japanese/Asian essence. Entering this space designed to
express the key words "fire, water, wood, earth and space" is
like entering another world.

●Restaurant

ニッポンビストロ デン
NIPPON BISTRO Den   Japan
東京都豊島区南池袋1-28-2 池袋PARCO 8F
8F Ikebukuro Parco, 1-28-2 Minami-Ikebukuro Toshima-ku Tokyo

A ： 窪田修一 Shuichi Kubota
AF： ㈱フィールドワーク Fieldwork Co., Ltd.
P ： ㈱パルコ プロモーション Parco Promotion Co., Ltd.
CW, DF: ㈱ミュー プランニング アンド オペレーターズ
　　　　 Myu & Operators Co., Ltd.

コースター　Coaster

「美味しければ、楽しければなんでもアリ」をコンセプトにしたレストランでは、リーズナブルなワインや創作料理をおしゃれな空間の中で楽しめる。グラフィックに日本の国旗に使用されている赤色と白色を配し、この店が日本風ビストロであることを印象づけている。

A Japanese pub-type restaurant serving reasonably priced wines and creative cuisine in a chic atmosphere where anything goes if it is fun and delicious. Red and white — referencing the Japanese flag — is used in the graphics to signal that the restaurant is a Japanese-style bistro.

モ〜モ〜パラダイス 新宿三丁目牧場
Mo-Mo-Paradise Japan
東京都新宿区新宿3-30-11 新宿高野第二ビル8F
8F Shinjuku Takano Daini-Bldg.,
3-30-11 Shinjuku Shinjuku-ku Tokyo

A：冨永俊三　Shunzo Tominaga
AF：㈱テトラ　Tetora

ショップカード　Shop Card

手ごろな値段で上質な牛肩ロースや自然農法の野菜を
使ったしゃぶしゃぶ、すき焼きの食べ放題を提供。年令
や性別に関係なく様々な層の顧客が集う場ということも
あり、落ち着いた和の空間を演出している。

A restaurant offering customers their fill of sukiyaki and shabu-
shabu made from top-quality beef and organically-grown
vegetables at a reasonable price. The calm Japanese-style
interior is designed to attract a wide range of customers.

手作り料理とお酒 えん　EN　Japan
東京都豊島区南池袋1-28-2 池袋パルコ8F
8F Ikebukuro Parco, 1-28-2 Minami-Ikebukuro Toshima-ku Tokyo

大人が満足できる和食居酒屋として、幅広い層から支持される店づくりを実現した飲食店。和食をベースとして素材にこだわった創作料理と、活気のあるオープンキッチンを見ることができるゆったりとした和の空間が魅力的。

A Japanese-style pub that satisfies adult taste supported by design attention applied on a variety of levels. Japanese-based cuisine made with select ingredients and a lively open kitchen add to the appeal of the spacious Japanese-style interior.

伊達鶏・野菜とお酒の すみか
Sumika　Japan
東京都武蔵野市吉祥寺本町1-8-10 吉祥寺ビルB1F
B1F Kichijoji-Bldg., 1-8-10 Kichijoji Hon-cho
Musashino-shi Tokyo

A：竹田直紀　Naoki Takeda
AF：㈱エム・ディー　MD Inc.

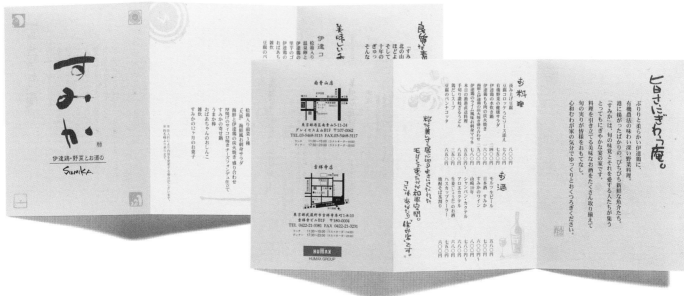

コースター　Coaster

竹で組まれたあじろ天井や、海底の粘土質で作られた土壁
など、店内の随所に天然素材を使用。バリ島にあるアマンダ
リというリゾートホテルをモチーフにデザインされた、伊
達鶏や自然農法の野菜を楽しめる和食レストランである。

A bamboo wickerwork ceiling, mud walls made with ocean-
bottom clay — every corner of the store interior is composed of
natural materials. A Japanese restaurant serving specially raised
chicken and organically-grown vegetables imaged after the Bali
resort hotel Amandari.

227

きた山　Kitayama　Japan

神奈川県横浜市港北区新横浜2-17-11 アイシスプラザ新横浜1F
2-17-11 Shinyokohama Kohoku-ku Yokohama-shi Kanagawa

A : 金子 裕　Hiroshi Kaneko
AF : ㈱山下設計 横浜支社
　　　　Yamashita Sekkei, Yokohama Office
CD, AD, D : 片野 勉　Ben Katano
P : 田辺隆三　Ryuzo Tanabe
DF : ㈲ベンカタノデザイン　Ben Katano Design, Inc.

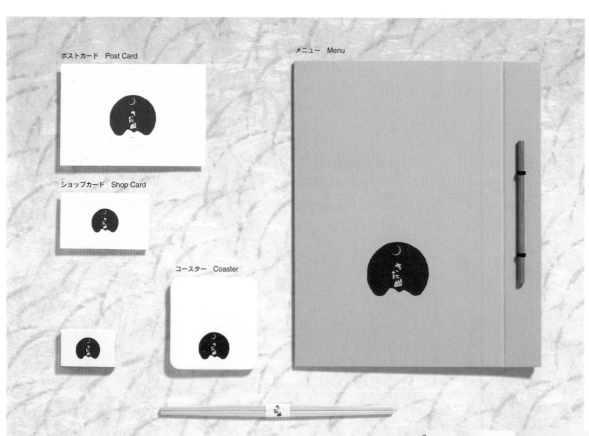

ポストカード　Post Card

ショップカード　Shop Card

コースター　Coaster

メニュー　Menu

日本の伝統的な素材を多用した純日本風のインテリアの
中、季節感あふれる日本料理が堪能できる店。ロゴマーク
は京都にある北山を連想させるものとし、グラフィック
もこれにマッチするよう、自然を感じさせる色づかいと
デザインになっている。

Seasonally inspired Japanese cuisine offered in a purely
Japanese-style interior using a variety of traditional Japanese
materials. The logomark alludes to Kyoto's Kitayama; the use
of color and design of the graphics express the same
sensibility of nature.

四季の旬菜料理 アエン　AEN　Japan
東京都目黒区自由が丘2-8-20
2-8-20 Jiyugaoka Meguro-ku Tokyo

ランチョンマット　Luncheon Mat

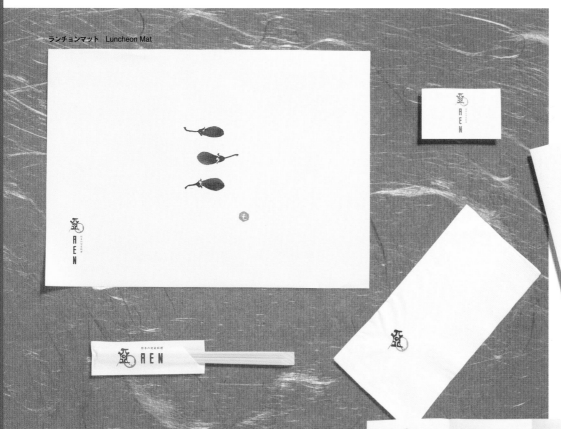

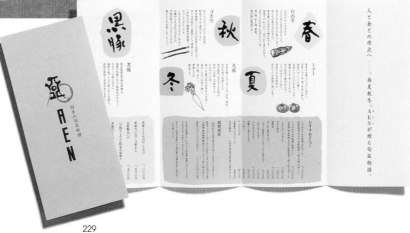

自然と人間が交流する「土間」と、大地が生み出してきた
「地球色」をコンセプトとして、店内およびグラフィック
のデザインがなされている旬菜料理の店。やすらぎを感
じる空間は、自然素材を使って演出されている。

Interior and graphic design for a Japanese restaurant
revolving around an earth-floor space, which represents the
exchange between people nature, and earth-tone colors.
Natural materials are used to create an atmosphere that
promotes peace of mind.

食の房 澁家　Shoku-no-bo Shibuya　Japan

東京都渋谷区渋谷1-16-14 メトロプラザ1F
1F Metro Plaza, 1-16-14 Shibuya Shibuya-ku Tokyo

A： 金子誉樹　Shigeki Kaneko
AF： ㈲スタジオ ムーン　Studio Moon
CD： 増田浩幸　Hiroyuki Masuda
D： 岡部 泉　Izumi Okabe
DF： ㈲イエローデータ Yellow Data / ㈲ヒロユキ Hiroyuki Inc.

ショップカード
Shop Card

メニュー　Menu

日本の風呂敷をアートとしてとらえ、店内の壁面にディスプレイするなど、個性的な演出が光るレストラン。新しい視点で取り入れられた「和」のイメージが、居酒屋でもありビストロでもあるという店のコンセプトを表現。

Japanese furoshiki (wrapping cloths) displayed on the walls as art contribute to the dramatic effect of this unique a restaurant. A new perspective of "wa" (Japanese aesthetics) expresses the combination izakaya (Japanese-style pub)/bistro concept.

まいど
Bistro de Maido Japan
東京都渋谷区渋谷1-10-12 宮城ビルB1F
B1F Miyagi-Bldg., 1-10-12 Shibuya Shibuya-ku Tokyo

A : 金子誉樹 Shigeki Kaneko
AF : ㈲スタジオ ムーン Studio Moon
CD : 増田浩幸 Hiroyuki Masuda
D : 岡部 泉 Izumi Okabe
DF : ㈲イエローデータ Yellow Data
㈲ヒロユキ Hiroyuki Inc.

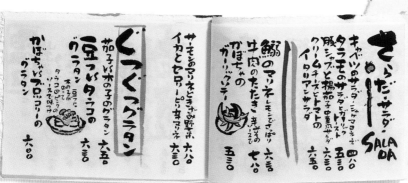

メニュー　Menu

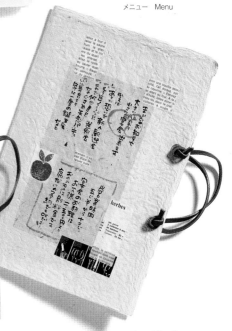

ショップカード
Shop Card

カジュアルな雰囲気の中で、和の食材を洋風にアレンジ
した料理を提供する和風ビストロ。店のイメージと統一
感を出すため、メニューや季節のDMに手書き文字を多
用するなど、ぬくもりを感じさせるグラフィックデザイ
ンを展開している。

A Japanese-style bistro offering Western-arranged dishes
using Japanese ingredients. Graphic devices, such
handwriting on the menus and direct-mail announcements,
unify the store image and express a sense of warmth.

Restaurant

ブラッセリー 給食当番
BRASSERIE Kyushoku Toban　Japan
東京都台東区元浅草1-4-4
1-4-4 Motoasakusa Taito-ku Tokyo

コースター　Coaster

メニュー　Menu

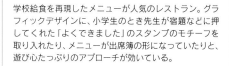

学校給食を再現したメニューが人気のレストラン。グラフィックデザインに、小学生のとき先生が宿題などに押してくれた「よくできました」のスタンプのモチーフを取り入れたり、メニューが出席簿の形になっていたりと、遊び心たっぷりのアプローチが効いている。

A popular "school lunch revival" restaurant. Menus imaged after a school attendance ledger, and graphics incorporating school grading symbols of merit as a motif — the playful spirit is well-received.

Index
of Submittors

作品提供者 ●

Submittors

Designer

野村恭子　Kyoko Nomura

Editor

近藤弘子　Hiroko Kondo

Photographer

藤本邦治　Kuniharu Fujimoto

Translators

パメラ・ミキ　Pamela Miki

Coordinator

飯島醇二　Junji Iijima

Typesetter

長谷川 豊　Yutaka Hasegawa

Publisher

三芳伸吾　Shingo Miyoshi

shop image graphics

ショップ イメージ グラフィックス

2000年12月14日初版第1刷発行

発行所　ピエ・ブックス
〒170-0003　東京都豊島区駒込4-14-6 #301
編集 Tel: 03-3949-5010 Fax: 03-3949-5650
　　　e-mail: editor@piebooks.com
営業 Tel: 03-3940-8302 Fax: 03-3576-7361
　　　e-mail: sales@piebooks.com

印刷・製本　図書印刷（株）

©2000 by P・I・E BOOKS

ISBN4-89444-145-4 C3070

Printed in Japan

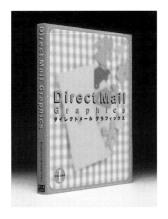

DIRECT MAIL GRAPHICS Vol.1
業種別世界のDMコレクション

Pages: 224 (Full Color) ¥15,534＋Tax

The long-awaited design collection featuring direct mailers with outstanding sales impact and quality design. 350 of the best pieces, classified into 100 business categories. A veritable textbook of current direct marketing design.

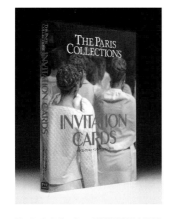

The Paris Collections / INVITATION CARDS
パリ・コレクションの招待状グラフィックス

Pages: 176 (Full Color) ¥13,398＋Tax

This book features 400 announcements for and invitations to the Paris Collections, produced by the world's top fashion brands over the past 10 years. A treasure trove of ideas and pure fun to browse through.

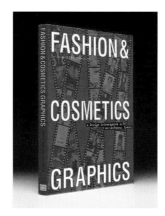

FASHION & COSMETICS GRAPHICS
世界のファション＆コスメティックのグラフィック特集

Pages: 208 (Full Color) ¥15,534＋Tax

We have published a collection of graphics from around the world produced for apparel, accessory and cosmetic brands at the vanguard of the fashion industry. A total of about 800 labels, tags, direct mailers, etc., from some 40 brands featured in this book point the way toward future trends in advertising.

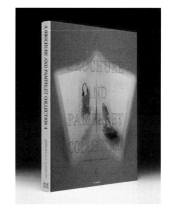

BROCHURE & PAMPHLET COLLECTION Vol.4
好評！業種別カタログ・コレクション、第4弾

Pages: 224 (Full Color) ¥15,534＋Tax

The fourth volume in our popular "Brochure & Pamphlet" series. Twelve types of businesses categories represented through artwork that really sells. This book conveys a sense of what's happening right now in the catalog design scene. A must for all creators.

EVENT FLYER GRAPHICS
世界のイベントフライヤー・コレクション

Pages: 224 (Full Color) ¥15,534＋Tax

Here's a special selection zooming in on flyers promoting events. This upbeat selection covers wide-ranging music events, as well as movies, exhibitions and the performing arts.

SEASONAL CAMPAIGN GRAPHICS
デパート・ショップのシーズン別キャンペーン広告特集

Pages: 224 (Full Color) ¥15,534＋Tax

A spirited collection of quality graphics for sales campaigns planned around the four seasons and Christmas, St. Valentine's Day and the Japanese gift-giving seasons, as well as for store openings, anniversaries, and similar events.

ADVERTISING FLYER GRAPHICS
衣・食・住・遊の商品チラシ特集

Pages: 224 (Full Color) ¥15,534＋Tax

The eye-catching flyers selected for this new collection represent a broad spectrum of businesses, and are presented in a loose classification covering four essential areas of modern life styles: fashion, dining, home and leisure.

PRESENTATION GRAPHICS
発想から完成までのプレゼンテーション特集

Pages: 192 (Full Color) ¥15,500＋Tax

31 creators from 8 countries illustrate the complete presentation process, from the first idea sketches and color comps, to presentations and the final result. We show you aspects of the design world that you've never seen before in this unique, invaluable book.

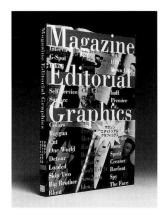

MAGAZINE EDITORIAL GRAPHICS
洗練された世界のエディトリアル・デザイン特集

Pages: 224 (Full Color) ¥15,500＋Tax

The stylish world of editorial and cover design in a new collection! English avant-garde, French new wave, American energy... 79 hot publications from 9 countries have been selected, all featuring the graphic works of top designers. A veritable New Age design bible.

NEW TYPOGRAPHICS Vol.2
世界の最新タイポグラフィックスをコレクション！

Pages: 224 (Full Color) ¥15,500＋Tax

The latest in international typographic design! Simple, modern design; stimulating visuals; experimental typography; creative yet readable styles... We bring you 400 exhilarating new works from countries that include Germany, Switzerland, the Netherlands, England, America, and Japan.

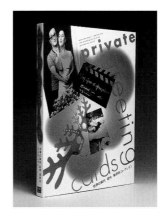

PRIVATE GREETING CARDS
季節の挨拶状、個人的な案内状・招待状の大特集

Pages: 224 (Full Color) ¥15,500＋Tax

A big, new collection of greetings, announcements, and invitations! Christmas, New Year's, and other seasonal cards; birth and moving announcements; invitations to weddings and exhibitions... 450 cards by designers around the world, even more fun just because they're private!

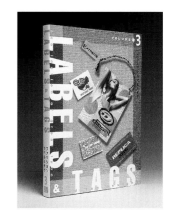

LABELS & TAGS Vol.3
最新ファッションブランドのラベル＆タグコレクション

Pages: 216 (Full Color) ¥15,500＋Tax

From ladies', men's, and unisex fashions, to kids' clothing, jeans, and sports brands, here are more than 1,000 unique labels and tags, classified by item. Expanding the possibilities of fashion graphics, this is the must-have book that designers have been waiting for!

MAGAZINE ADVERTISING GRAPHICS
業種別 世界の独創的な雑誌広告デザイン特集

Pages: 224 (Full Color) ¥13,500+Tax

Conceptual, distinctively original magazine ads, selected from 19 countries for their novel, high-impact visuals and attention-grabbing copy (Japanese and English translations provided where copy is essential to the ad's effectiveness). All are model examples of successful promotion production.

CATALOG GRAPHICS
衣・食・住のセールスカタログ特集

Pages: 224 (Full Color) ¥13,500+Tax

Here you will find hundreds of practical catalogs and pamphlets, all designed to SELL. Including product descriptions and pictures, prices and options, even order forms, this is an essential collection for anyone seeking ways to stimulate the consumers' desire to buy.

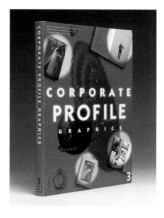

CORPORATE PROFILE GRAPHICS Vol.3
大好評！世界の会社案内グラフィックス、第3弾

Pages: 224 (Full Color) ¥13,500+Tax

The latest catalogs from companies, schools, and facilities around the world. Covers as well as selected inside pages of 200 high-quality catalogs are included, allowing full enjoyment of concepts and layout. Arranged by industry.

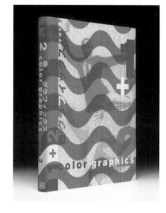

1＋2 COLOR GRAPHICS Vol.2
大好評！効果的な1&2色デザインの大特集、第2弾

page: 224 (Full Color) ¥13,500+Tax

The works presented here have all been selected for their effective use of one, or at most, two, colors. Presenting fresh, new ways of combining colors this book shows that by limiting the number of colors the possibilities of design can in fact be expanded.

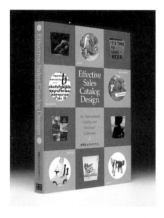

EFFECTIVE SALES CATALOG DESIGN
効果的な世界のセールス・カタログ特集

Pages: 224 (Full Color) ¥13,500+Tax

A special international collection of effective sales catalogs. The more than 200 beautifully designed catalogs found here include prices and sizes, features and product descriptions, all of the information that is vital to the consumer. Categorized by product, this one volume is packed full of ideas for the catalog designer.

SUCCESSFUL DIRECT MAIL DESIGN Vol.2
大好評！ セールス効果の高いDM特集、第2弾

Pages: 224 (Full Color) ¥13,500+Tax

By popular demand! Volume 2 of our Effective DM series. You'll find more than 500 examples of direct mail from all over the world, designed for a wide range of businesses to help them increase sales. This is a book that simply explodes with energy, clearly revealing the passion the designers have for their work. Categorized by business for quick reference.

NEW POSTCARD GRAPHICS
SEASONAL ANNOUNCEMENTS
季節の案内状：年賀状・暑中見舞・クリスマスカード特集

Pages: 192 (Full Color) ¥9,800+Tax

New Year's, Summer Greetings, Christmas Card Edition. "Seasonal greetings" is the theme of this collection of more than 800 postcards, all of which are noteworthy for their exceptional design. Readers will be entranced by the variety of design essence that can fit within the limited dimensions of a postcard. An outstanding collection overflowing with unique works.

ADVERTISING PHOTOGRAPHY IN JAPAN 2000
年鑑　日本の広告写真2000

Pages: 240 (Full Color) ¥14,500+Tax

With editorial supervision by the Japan Advertising Photographers' Association, this year's annual contains 409 works selected from the very best Japanese advertising photography of 1997-98. These photos, which collectively create a portrait of our time, will attract much attention as a piece of photographic history.

NEW BUSINESS CARD GRAPHICS Vol.2
大好評の名刺コレクション、さらに充実した第2弾

Pages: 224 (Full Color) ¥12,000+Tax

A new and even more comprehensive volume of our popular business card series. More than 850 selections, ranging from designers' own namecards, to corporate business cards, to restaurant and shop cards. You will find simple and chic designs, as well as those both pop and hyper. Cards are divided into four design categories. A book packed with ideas.

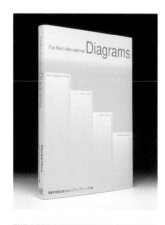

THE BEST INFORMATIONAL DIAGRAMS
情報を視覚化したビジュアル・グラフィック集

Pages: 224 (Full Color) ¥13,500+Tax

Charts, graphs, maps, pictograms, medical and architectural illustrations, and more! A myriad of information translated into easy-to-grasp graphics. This superb collection boasts 350 diagrams from all over the world, all designed for effective and clear communication.

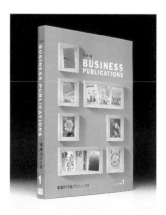

NEW BUSINESS PUBLICATIONS 1
大好評の業種別PR誌の特集、第三弾

Pages: 224 (Full Color) ¥13,500+Tax

The third volume in our popular PR publications series! More than 130 select informational booklets and community newspapers categorized by business. With covers and inside pages of each issue presented to show the flow of their underlying concepts and plans, this single volume is an invaluable practical reference.

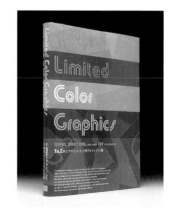

LIMITED COLOR GRAPHICS
1&2色でデザインした小型グラフィック集

Pages: 224 (Full Color) ¥13,500+Tax

A collection of 1- and 2-color direct mailers, flyers and other small-scale collateral materials that have no less impact than their 4-color competition. Each work is presented along with swatches and Pantone numbers of the ink colors used as well as swatches of the stock colors.

New Postcard Graphics / SALES POSTCARD DESIGN
効果絶大なセール案内のポストカード特集

Pages: 192 (Full Color)　¥9,800＋Tax

An all-inclusive collection of sale announcement postcards that pack a punch! An entire volume focusing on sale announcements, the area of direct-mail marketing in greatest demand. Postcards announcing department and other store sales, restaurant menu changes, and new skin care products categorized by industry for easy reference.

NEW COMPANY BROCHURE DESIGN
最新 業種別（会社・学校・施設）案内カタログ特集

Pages: 240 (Full Color)　¥15,000＋Tax

A collection of the latest brochures from companies, schools and institutions. Over 200 brochures displaying high-quality design expressing superb concepts and planning. With pages featuring corporate philosophies reproduced at a readable scale, this single volume is a sourcebook of brochure concepts and design ideas.

LIMITED RESOURCES / LIMITLESS CREATIVITY
制約をプラスに変えるアイデア作品集

Pages: 208 (Full Color) ¥13,500＋Tax

A collection of works based on ideas that turn limitations into creative advantages. Low budget/high impact promotional pieces, packaging that brings out the best of natural materials, highly individual playfully devised announcements and invitations—more than 200 unique works presented with their design concepts. The ideas on each page of this volume are as innovative as the next.

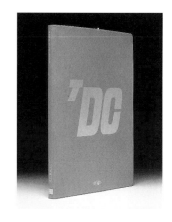

THE TOKYO TYPE DIRECTORS CLUB ANNUAL 2000
最先端のタイポグラフィーとディレクション作品を満載

Pages: 252 (234 in Color) ¥14,500＋Tax

Packed with cutting-edge typography and type direction; the most outstanding works of the year selected in Japan's only international graphic design competition–the renowned The Tokyo Type Directors Club Annual (TDC) Award. This year's annual–for the commemorative year 2000–documents the entire array of the superb awarding-winning and honorary-mention works.

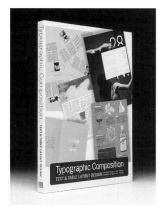

TYPOGRAPHIC COMPOSITION: TEXT & TABLE LAYOUT DESIGN
シンプルで美しい文字レイアウトと表組デザインの大特集

Pages: 224 (Full Color) ¥13,000＋Tax

The finest examples of typographic composition from a variety of printed media—including company profiles, catalogs, magazines, and books—grouped in four basic categories: table of contents, primarily text pages, captions/supplementary text on primarily visual pages, and tables. An indispensable layout design reference.

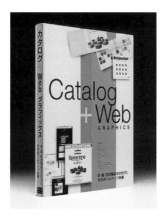

CATALOG + WEB GRAPHICS
デザインの優れたカタログ＆Webを一挙掲載

Pages: 304 (Full Color) ¥15,000＋Tax

Exceptional catalog and website design compiled in one volume! Over 70 catalogs, pamphlets and corresponding webpages designed to promote sales, categorized by their product's relation to the subjects "food, clothes, and shelter." Both the print and web pages are presented on the same spread to facilitate comparison of how these superb designs translate in the different mediums.

ピエ・ブックス

〒170-0003　東京都豊島区駒込4-14-6-301

P·I·E BOOKS

#301, 4-14-6 komagome, Toshima-ku, Tokyo 170-0003 JAPAN

カタログ・新刊のご案内について

総合カタログ、新刊案内をご希望の方は、はさみ込みのアンケートはがきを
ご返送いただくか、90円切手同封の上、ピエ・ブックス宛お申し込みください。

CATALOGS and INFORMATION ON NEW PUBLICATIONS

If you would like to receive a free copy of our general catalog
or details of our new publications, please fill out the enclosed postcard
and return it to us by mail or fax.

CATALOGUES ET INFORMATIONS SUR LES NOUVELLES PUBLICATIONS

Si vous désirez recevoir un exemplaire gratuit de notre catalogue généralou des
détails sur nos nouvelles publication. veuillez compléter la carte réponse incluse et
nous la retourner par courrierou par fax.

CATALOGE und INFORMATIONEN ÜBER NEUE TITLE

Wenn Sie unseren Gesamtkatalog oder Detailinformationen über
unsere neuen Titel wünschen.fullen Sie bitte die beigefügte Postkarte aus
und schicken Sie sie uns per Post oder Fax.

ピエ・ブックス

〒170-0003　東京都豊島区駒込4-14-6-301
TEL : 03-3940-8302　FAX: 03-3576-7361

P·I·E BOOKS

#301, 4-14-6 komagome, Toshima-ku, Tokyo 170-0003 JAPAN
TEL : +81-3-3940-8302 FAX : +81-3-3576-7361